To t

A story of loss but also
one of so many memories...
With best wishes,
Nina

FOUR DAYS IN JANUARY
A LETTER TO JILLSAN

Four Days in January

A LETTER TO JILLSAN

✦

Nils-Johan Jørgensen

RENAISSANCE BOOKS

FOUR DAYS IN JANUARY
A LETTER TO JILLSAN
by Nils-Johan Jørgensen

First published 2009 by Renaissance Books

Renaissance Books is an imprint of
Global Books Ltd
PO Box 219, Folkestone, Kent CT20 2WP, UK

© Nils-Johan Jørgensen 2009

ISBN 978-1-898823-01-8

British Library Cataloguing in Publication Data
A CIP catalogue entry for this book is available
from the British Library

Set in Garamond 11 on 13pt by Mark Heslington, Scarborough, North Yorkshire
Printed and bound in England by Athenaeum Press, Gateshead, Tyne and Wear

For Lily

Suddenly there came a messenger
Who told me she was dead —
Was gone like a yellow leaf of autumn.
Dead as the day dies with the setting sun,
Lost as the bright moon is lost behind the cloud,
Alas, she is no more, whose soul
Was bent to mine like the bending seaweed!

When the word was brought to me
I knew not what to do nor what to say;
But restless at the mere news,
And hoping to heal my grief
Even a thousandth part,
I journeyed to Karu and searched the market-place
Where my wife was wont to go!

There I stood and listened.
But no voice of her I heard,
Though the birds sang in the Unebi Mountain;
None passed by who even looked like my wife.
I could only call her name and wave my sleeve.

Kakinomoto no Hitomaro, 'After the Death of His Wife'.*

Memories have no future; they can only visit the past and return like the restless sea to the shore.

(Sensei)

---

* Kakinomoto no Hitomaro (about 665–715). His poetry is included in the *Manyōshū* . He was honoured by the title *kasei* (saint of poetry) and ranks as one of the greatest poets in Japanese literature. *1000 Poems from the Manyōshū*, Dover Editions, 2005, 42.

ONE

✦

Jill,

W hen is your birthday?' I asked. And you looked at me one last time and whispered the date of our wedding day.

You had seen the snow-white rose of paradise, touched the gold of the eternal rose; 'and she, so distant fled, it seemed, did smile and look on me once more, then to the eternal fountain turned her head'.[1]

My beautiful English Rose, my brave girl, the promised end came so suddenly. But as you would say, 'tell me all from the beginning'. Yes, my love, but it is the saddest of all tales.

It seemed like a normal day. I had taken Monty, the Serengeti boxer as we used to call him, for a walk. When I got back you said: 'I slept so badly last night.'

You and I sat together at the breakfast table as Nina walked in having just returned to England from the Special Court for Sierra Leone in Freetown. She was early and greeted us with a bright smile. I got up to hug her. Strangely, you remained seated, but then you got up very slowly.

We started to talk excitedly to Nina but something was troubling you. You wanted to know all about Nina's journey starting

1

from Lungi airport but then you began to ask strange questions and mixed unconnected words into your sentences. I asked: 'What is wrong?'

Three weeks earlier we had returned from Freetown having visited Nina. Was this the onset of cerebral malaria? I even hoped so but a fear filled my heart. Could this be more serious? You first tried to laugh it off but then you went quiet. Nina and I had to react, and react quickly. I led you through to the sitting room. You did not seem to respond or to register what was happening around you. We decided to drive directly to Queen Elizabeth The Queen Mother Hospital in Margate. We had no time to wait for an ambulance. You were able to get yourself ready, but as you came through into the kitchen you looked at your slippers and said, 'I can't go in these.'

You were so hauntingly silent on the journey. When I asked if this was the right way you simply pointed but said nothing. When we walked into the hospital I held your hand. In the waiting room the television was on. It was showing a rendering of *Do not go gentle into that good night*.[2] How strange and disturbing. It felt like a warning of what was to come, like a distant drum. But we would rage against the dying of your light. We registered and you were quickly transferred for examination.

A process started with questions you had to answer to determine a diagnosis. You were at first able to respond, even repeating the doctor's phonetic mistake, pronouncing w as v. You said my name, but when asked where you lived you said 'Bonn, Dar' (two cities where we had lived). The test deteriorated quickly. How unreal and ominous it sounded, like an echo from another world, when you began to answer questions with numbers. What was happening to you? Perhaps we knew but how could we face the reality unfolding?

Suddenly there was heightened activity and a rush. You were taken for a scan. The young Registrar recruited from South Africa came out with the result. With a look of pained sorrow she said: 'There has been a bleed, it is serious.'

It was a massive intracerebral haemorrhage.

You seemed to be fading away but still you kept fighting back, struggling to hold on to life. You smoothed Nina's hair frantically and straightened her collar. Nina asked you if you knew her name and you looked as if to say, of course, but then you said 'Dilly' (a nickname for Lisa).

An evaluation followed and contact was made with King's College Hospital in London to prepare for a possible operation. I was asked to go with you in the ambulance but after intense consultations with two specialists in London medical wisdom concluded that there was no point and no hope. And there was no intensive care bed available.

We kept clinging on to fragments of hope but one by one they were dashed. The medical staff kept taking us into 'the bad news room' each time chance faded further. The decision not to operate closed the door.

It is strange to think that you walked into the hospital that morning but the collective and best medical knowledge in the world could not save you. 'Love's moment in a world in servitude to time.'[3] I knew then that I would not walk out from there with you and hold your hand again but I still did not want to believe that there was no return.

The hospital looked after you as your body fought and fought but the tsunami in your brain had destroyed you. The bright mind that got A-Distinction at A-level was taken away. I would now carry your consciousness, your soul.

Nina had immediately informed Lisa who was living in Italy of the seriousness of the situation but the airports were closed because of snow and it seemed impossible to get out quickly. Everything seemed to be colluding against us.

Lisa, Richard and Lily eventually made it to England. Lisa carried your seven-week-old grandson in her womb. We were all around you. Only the hope of miracle remained, a fading flicker against all hope. 'Ne me quitte pas.'[4]

And then a final remarkable life force came through against all odds. Your eyes had long since closed but I gently held them open and told you: 'Look, we are all here. Nina, Lisa, Lily, Richard and I.'

Somehow you moved your eyes and your heart seemed to open to us as we stood bowed by the bed. You made this quiet but intense breath sound like a last farewell as if you wanted to say: 'I don't want to leave you. Thank you, thank you, thank you for our moments together.' 'Your voice was ever soft, gentle and low.'[5]

Throughout the vigil Lisa and Nina gave sorrow words as they searched for meaning in written messages of love. Each tear divided into a thousand tears.

I realized then that I had never before really known tears:

> Before, I knew nothing of tears,
> as I passed along this small stretch of life.
> The old stories of long, long ago
> I learned with no sense of their sorrows.
>   But now that my love has gone away,
> gone and truly left me,
> everything I had thought was mine
> has slipped away, now is lost.
>   Only those stories I learned long ago,
> those alone remain with me.[6]

We held your hand in benediction over you. How little we know of the mystery of life. New research suggests that the damaged brain still has an internal life and may register, hear and understand but is unable to respond. Perhaps deep brain activity made you aware of your surroundings. How much did you know, how much did you perceive and feel as the towering wave overwhelmed you?

The Registrar came in one last time on the final day and said: 'This is what happens when it is terminal,' describing your breathing.

Lisa said, 'it is still Mummy,' and the doctor replied, 'she will always be your mother.' Then the doctor could not hold back her own tears and had to rush out of the room.

Then you turned towards the crystal fountain and a day later your last heart beat and your last breath took you away to the lands beyond the seas. 'The soul driven from the body mourns the memory it leaves behind.'[7] Lisa and Nina cried in unison: 'Mummy, Mummy, Mummy.' Then suddenly everything went still.

'Pray you undo this button ... Look there, look there!'[8] But the luck had run out. You had slipped to eternity. Life leaked away. The last examination. The wine of life was drawn. Your soul took wings like a dream takes wings. The wheel of fortune had turned into a wheel of fire. The fire and the rose were one. 'Never, never, never, never, never!'[9]

The light had gone out of my life and it seemed that the whole world was widowed by your death.[10]

The phoenix will not arise and fly again, the shrine cannot be rebuilt.[11] But the gods themselves threw incense. Lily, so young, had witnessed it all. She waved and whispered: 'Bye, bye.' Then very quietly she took a rose, the colour of a ripe apricot, and softly scattered petals over her grandmother and continued a trail to the door so that Mumbelle (as she called her then and ever after) could follow us back home.

We went back to Wychway. Drive slowly; we will get there soon enough.[12] We were deracinated. The face of sorrow. Can we face anything except a deep sorrow? 'Mi ritrovai per una selva oscura che la diritta via era smaritta.'[13] The trees and the house seemed eerily empty.

Quietly, Richard prepared a meal, provided ballast. To feel hungry is a symptom of shock. It was a reminder that life must go on. We had promises to keep.

I opened the bottle of wine from 1966 saved for our wedding anniversary. We drank it in a spirit of communion. We sat in an eternal circle to select music for the Chapel of Remembrance. We had to prepare for your final journey. We found an elegant dress for you. You always had perfect style. We saw you one last time, dressed and still for the journey to the undiscovered country. We were silent.

You came back one last time to Old Road; to the house you had found and made into our home where all the souvenirs from seven countries and miles of travelling had finally settled down. Now you were confined in a coffin visible only through the glass of the hearse with soft petalled apricot roses on top. It seemed unreal. Life is not fair.

We drove slowly through the village, the funeral director walking in front. We passed the windmill and then we set out for Thanet Crematorium. On the way we drove past Kent International Airport, Manston, famous from the days of the Battle of Britain and a reminder of your years of flying. The silhouettes of the aircraft seemed darkly to prepare for your last flight without return.

Your family had arrived in Kent in 1066 with the legendary William Taillefer who rode out in front at the Battle of Hastings. King William II rewarded the family and granted to the Lord of the Castle of Taillefer in Angoulême a property in St. Wenn in Cornwall. The property was given the name Borlase which means green pastures in Cornish. Now you were to rest in green pastures 'far away into the silent land'.[14]

The Chapel of Remembrance is set in a spacious garden with reflections of Japanese design. The weeping willows stood bare and the winter cherry petals were falling.

The Reverend Eric J. Powe reflected on the inner and outer journey that we all travel and we played the music we had selected for you. A memorial plaque was later mounted at the Chapel and your name listed in the Book of Remembrance.

We went to the R.A.F. Manston Hurricane and Spitfire Memorial Building and Museum. We had a cup of tea. And so we were alone without you. As Lisa said, we had been four wheels that kept moving through time zones. Now one wheel of the chariot was forever missing. There had been a time for us.

We received so many words of sympathy and compassion – from north and south, east and west. The common theme was the unreality that the incredibly vital, vivacious, warm and generous Jill had passed away.

Your cousin in the USA reminded us of your early spirit: 'When we were kids Joy and I were always in awe of our city cousin because she would travel to Penrith on her own by train and even change at Crewe. I guess she was confident and worldly at the age of eight. One word can describe Jill, and that is, she was a lady in every sense.'

From the Embassy in Dar es Salaam came a card from all the staff with their warm messages and signed names.

A friend reflected on how fickle life can be. One moment everything is going according to plan then it is turned upside down in the most horrible way. He ended his letter with the words, *courage, mon brave.*

Friends from the International Forum in Oslo (where you had been the editor) wrote movingly about 'our dear Jill, enthusiastic, considerate, wise, friendly and humorous'.

When I told one friend what had happened to you she said nothing, only her eyes filled with tears.

Words also came to Lisa and Nina. You always had such rapport with young people. One of Lisa's close friends simply wrote: 'There is something of her wondrous spirit and smile that has stayed with me. All I can say is, wow, what a truly wonderful woman. How blessed you all were.'

We set up a memorial fund with a view to improve our understanding of the condition that you had suffered. We had a meeting with Professor Neil Kitchen at the Brain Research Trust.

□

The urn – formed like a box and delicately finished with your name engraved on top – was delivered to the house by the funeral director. I held a shrine in my hands. This was the most sacrosanct.

I travelled with you one last time from the white cliffs of Dover to the white nights of Bremnes. We held a memorial service at Hans Egedes Minne at Ytre Elgsnes.[15] I had made contact with the priest that we all had come to admire and respect, Lars Martin Skipevåg, and the service was set for 10 June. The urn was placed in front of the altar together with your picture and an apricot bunch. I carried a red rose and I put it down next to your picture. People assembled.

'Preludium' by Bach. Introduction and speech by Skipevåg, a tribute to Jill's life, compassionate, sympathetic, understanding. This slight, bearded friar had the ability to absorb our grief, inhaling it and lifting our burden. Lisa said he reminded her of a character in an early Renaissance fresco.

A relative said afterwards: 'There was so much I did not know about Jill.' 'Amazing Grace'. Then the abiding words by Lisa and Nina.

Lisa talked about your extraordinary ability to give us eight remarkable homes and in a matter of days the atmosphere would belong to us: 'I wonder if you might have seen angels, if you arrived at a place – your new home. You died so gracefully, without a moment of self-pity. You would have been carried by those angels and your smile. We are your barefoot children, your bears. Mummy's book will always be open.' Yes, you *set up homes inside our dreams.*[16]

'Do not be afraid,' said Nina, 'you are allowed to believe in the light above the mountain. When you climb we will hold your hands. Do not think our grip will loosen because you climb faster.'

These were words written in the dark hours when you were dying, words that held a candle to your life and your spirit. 'A mother's death must be something unique, unlike anything else, and must awaken inconceivable emotions within us.'[17] Love beyond imagination.

Richard read, 'Where the Wild Things are', a favourite story for Lisa and Nina and now for Lily from the same booklet you gave them thirty years ago. Lily went to sit next to your shrine and picture. Adagio from 'Clarinet Concerto in A-major' by Mozart.

Time for my words. What do I say when words fail? 'Gently they go, the beautiful, the tender, the kind; quietly they go, the intelligent, the witty, the brave. I know. But I do not approve. And I am not resigned.'[18] I read a most beautiful love poem in our culture, *Der König in Thule.* You gave me '... *einen goldnen Becher'* – a cup of gold.

Flight over Africa.[19] Prayer. And then *Con te partiro.*[20] I will go with you on ships across seas that I know exist no longer. I will go with you. *Postludium* by Bach *'Bist du bei mir'.*

We walked to the churchyard. I lowered the urn. We had put our final messages inside. The shrine is now fixed between our mountain and our sea, adorned by rocks and pines. I placed a Japanese lantern on your grave and lit a candle. Lily warmed her hands. Later a memorial stone cut out of the rock with your name and family motto (*Te digna sequere*) was added to the lantern. 'Abide with me'. Wait for me.

I said to Lily: 'I often hold your hand but today you held mine. Thank you.' One day you will understand: 'A very small hand came, peacefully holding mine. It was such a small hand ... holding my withered fingers in innocent grasp.'[21]

We gathered in 'Gjertrudstua' in *Hans Egedes Minne*. Uncle Thomas spoke movingly about Jill.

The rain had stopped and the sun appeared. I sent a silent semaphore towards the unchartered lands beyond the seas. Perhaps your journey took you to *makáron násos*, the island where golden flowers grow or to *wadatsumi*, the realm of brightness and abundance far off to the sea? We can no more hoist the spinnaker together and sail towards the midnight sun but I shall sail with a north wind and anchor my boat at the sea's edge. You are 'a thousand winds that blow'.[22]

As we left the sacred space and moved slowly towards the mountain road, a fox appeared and seemed to invite us to stop. He was cautious but friendly and he eagerly appreciated the cake we gave him from our hands. I was reminded that fox figures guard the *jinja* (shrine) of the rice god Inari. A strange Shinto symbolism, a sign that your *tama* (soul) and spirit remained to bless and protect us?

The Floating Bridge of Heaven (the rainbow) had now appeared over the sea after the rain. In early Verdic religion, that inspired Buddhism, destiny after death was believed to be in the hands of the descendants and the person who had passed away would reach an afterlife as a star in heaven.

I urged the old globetrotting Peugeot, shipped to Zimbabwe for our posting and then returned to Norway, up the steep and narrow road, cut into the vertical mountainside, a road refusing not to be there. You did not always like the road – rocks would sometimes fall – but how you loved the view.

We moved slowly in this familiar car that you used to drive Lisa and Nina in to Chisipite Junior School as they revised words for the daily spelling test in the back seat. Your granddaughter was now sitting in the same seat. Hairs from our adventurous boxer were still woven into the seats. It was always such a happy car, because it was your car. Its special blue colour made us think of spring and summer skies.

□

'We are such stuff as dreams are made on.'[23] I dreamt one night that you and I were together at the theatre. I left to buy a programme. When I returned I could not find you. The theatre had disappeared and I walked through dark streets to find my way back to you. I asked passers-by where the theatre was, but nobody knew.

In another dream we stood together at the quay. I went onboard a ship and suddenly it sailed away and I could not stop it. 'Where are you? I can't reach you.'

In a new dream I was in Japan at a reception with many people and suddenly you appeared in a beautiful dress, smiling and full of life with your long chestnut hair flying. But you seemed injured down the left side of your face and you carried a big round plaster over the injury. Then spontaneously you took it off and everything was fine. The scene sparkled with colour and life as your smile lit up the room. I then had to leave and I lost my way in Tokyo, unable to find the way back to you. 'Had I known my love's visit was but a dream I should never have awakened.'[24]

These dreams seemed to reflect the ancient legend and myth of Orpheus and Eurydice. Orpheus who had superhuman skills in music and song had descended to Hades in an attempt to restore his wife Eurydice to life. His music had charmed the gods of the underworld and he was allowed to return to earth with Eurydice provided he did not look back to see her until they reached the earth. But wanting irresistibly to see her face he looked back too soon and she was lost forever.[25]

We had so many incredible years but not days enough. Every moment with you was the best of times. 'Compar'd to this, All honor's mimique; All wealth alchimie.'[26]

You and I had faced the uneven road together:

Where others' husbands ride on horseback along the Yamashiro road, you, my husband, trudge on foot. Every time I see you there I weep, to think of it my heart aches. My husband, take on your back my shining mirror, my mother's keepsake, together with the scarf thin as the dragon-fly's wing, and barter them for a horse, I pray you, my husband.

If I get a horse, my beloved, you must go on foot; though we tread the rocks, let's walk, the two of us, together![27]

We travelled and trod North and South, East and West together. Our time had stopped. I stopped the hands of the big clock in the hall at Seven, that is, at Nineteen. You were nineteen when I first saw you; it is the date of our wedding day and your last words. I attached the key from the urn at the tip of the long hand. Were the gods envious? 'The perplexity of mankind, who can give no answer.'[28]

On the day you died, the postman left a letter confirming that the manuscript for my book on Germany and Japan subtitled *The Spirit of Renewal* had been accepted for publication. It was like a sign from you from beyond the stars, a spirit still supporting and encouraging the way you always did. 'And a whisper will be heard in the place where the ruined house once stood.'[29]

We walked up Wrefords Lane in Exeter one Summer's day. We had the time between that day and those four days in January. There is never a time to say goodbye. If only you could come back, the way you always did from your journeys, now, wouldn't that be something?

Someday we will lie side by side, hold hands and tell old stories from the beginning – at least I am permitted to imagine that. We found 'the love that moves the sun and the other stars'.[30]

Her name was Jill. She was my girl.

TWO

✦

When I had written these first lines you seemed to implore me: 'Tell me more. What happened? What did you feel and think? What did you do?'

So let me continue this final letter to you.

After the memorial ceremony, I arrived at the timber cottage by the sea at midnight, our *Byaku Ya*[1] that you and I had built between rocks and trees like a Shinto shrine, a refuge for two travellers who held hands through time zones.

I passed the two Japanese lanterns set between stones, gravel and moss in the garden. A light easterly wind touched the sea. Two oyster catchers greeted me in low flight, their wings just missing the sea's surface; two seagulls circled and landed as two small whales surfaced for air. A cormorant sat motionless on a boulder, its dark wings ominously outstretched. 'What happiness can I wish you in your death?'[2]

I watched the dance of the waters. 'My longing for her is a thousand waves that roll from the sea each day.'[3]

I unlocked and opened the door, drew the curtains. '*Tis the yeares midnight.*[4] The midnight sun kept me company as I followed our routines to open the rooms after the dark winter. There was still snow on the mountains, but the sun held a promise of spring. I took the covers off the sofa, folded them and put them away. I walked slowly through the rooms. Everything was as you had left it. Above the blue fan from Kyoto with the image of the rising phoenix, I looked at your picture: stillness is the word of sorrow.

I opened the window and let the sound of the sea intensify the silence.

The two cherry trees I had planted were in white flower and petals fell as I took the few steps down to the sea's edge. 'Cherry blossoms that are blown off by the wind must feel reluctant to leave. What must I do with my feelings of longing to savour spring?'[5]

☐

As I looked across the sea I remembered the story of the cruel sea, the storm that had changed everything long ago. Lava Kristine had sailed with her two small daughters, Anna Karoline and Johanna Margrethe, to visit her parents while her husband had gone away to make their living from a generous sea. It was the darkest time of the year when the sun had not yet reappeared, *mørketid*,[6] the polar night. After a week she set out for home again but half way there a sudden gust, *kastevind*,[7] capsized the boat and they were lost forever. Only one of her shoes, which had been her bridal shoe, was ever found. She was married to my great grandfather. Many years later he remarried.[8]

Did they have to die so that I could get life? Now, how fair is that?

The sea seemed to embrace the large boulders below me. Let these giant dark stones, shaped by the endless sea, be their cenotaph and their shrine. 'If we had a keen vision and feeling of all ordinary human life ... we should die of that roar which lies on the other side of silence.'[9]

☐

My grief, cold and moist like water,[10] is calm tonight, like the sea after a perfect storm has created a giant wave, capsized the boat and sent it downwards to the deep and darkness. Then, slowly, the surface settles again into a restless calm as the waves in endless movements reach towards the land.

At a temple there once was a poem called 'Loss' carved into the stone. It had three words but the poet had scratched them out. You cannot read loss, only feel it.[11]

Against the midnight sun that can turn the sea and sky into light champagne, I see your young face, smiling and whispering: 'Come with me.' 27 June was the day we looked at the world for the first time together – the beginning, the first spiritual encounter, when our two souls met. Was it long ago or just yesterday? You wanted us to die together but it seemed unlikely that fate would grant us that honour: '... the soul that was born to die for you.'[12] We both knew that. The prize and price of love inseparable:

> When I die, I want your hands on my eyes:
> I want the light and wheat of your beloved hands
> to pass their freshness over me once more:
> I want to feel the softness that changed my destiny.
>
> I want you to live while I wait for you, asleep.
> I want your ears still to hear the wind, I want you
> to sniff the sea's aroma that we loved together,
> to continue to walk on the sand we walk on.
>
> I want what I love to continue to live,
> and you whom I love and sang above everything else
> to continue to nourish, full-flowered:
>
> so that you can reach everything my love directs you to,
> so that my shadow can travel along in your hair,
> so that everything can learn the reason for my song.[13]

But it was not to be. Instead, I had to put my hands over your beloved eyes. 'My only god in the days that were.'[14]

The sorrow of losing you divides into a first sorrow and a second sorrow. At first it was the immediate sense of losing the girl I married, who gave birth to our daughters and who made homes in eight countries. But then I found myself back at the beginning of our life, the first tender moments, the rays of youth. In my mind I am losing my beautiful, young sweetheart; what you were then. I am alone in this.

The focus and images in my mind are suddenly from the early days when I first met you and the time immediately afterwards. I am unable to let them go. 'I am tossed by sea and wind.'[15] You are every age in which I knew you, unchanged by time, but to remember you the way you were those summer days, and to remember you with such intense clarity, your beauty and elegance, your face, tender, fragile and mysterious, 'thine own fair eyes wherein I see myself',[16] your mouth, the tumbling, chestnut hair flowing over your shoulders, your perfect, graceful body, your breasts, and your long, slender, dancing legs, 'delicate as a crane',[17] your courage and whip-smart brightness, smile and voice, put me in a state beyond tears, a frozen knowledge that I can now only find you in memory. My soul is tormented in a soundless pain as the scenes change on the stage of our early life and then fuse into the whole life you gave me.

Death is the sum of what it steals from us. 'Tout ce que la mort ôtera est dans sa nuit ... Ce sont tous les plaisirs du monde qui se retirent en nous disant adieu' (All that death shall take away is in its night ... They are all the pleasures of this world that are taking their leave, bidding us adieu). [18] Each day dawns but once. You were six years younger than me. You should have lived.

When you died, the triadic pattern – past, present and future – was broken. There was no golden age in the future, no *apokatastasis*, no renewal. 'Although every year the plum bursts in bloom again I live in a world hollow as a locust shell where spring does not return.'[19] The past was locked into the present without a future rebirth because I was alone without you. You were the future, the golden age.

Memories have no future; they can only visit the past and return like the restless sea to the shore.

Was it chance, coincidence only, or destiny that our roads crossed and we met? Chance, as arbitrary as when the boat capsized a long time ago? But that sudden *kastevind* made you and me, our destiny, possible.

□

I attended a lecture by Professor Lord David Cecil, at the University of Oxford in 1961 on the concept of tragedy. 'What is tragedy?' mused the Professor. His point was that the essence of tragedy was the consequences of a death for the living. But is that not to forget what the deceased has been and is missing by no longer living?

> When you died
> I did not for the moment
> think about myself;
> I grieved deeply and purely for your loss,
> that you had lost your life.
> I grieved bitterly for your mind destroyed,
> your courage thrown away,
> your senses aborted under the amazing skin
> no one would ever touch again.[20]

After the death of his wife the cognitive scientist Douglas Hofstadter made the same point: What had hit him by far the hardest was not his own personal loss but his wife's personal loss. Her future, once so easily taken for granted, was lost in a flash.[21] No future time.

When people, in well meaning sentiment, insist that I have wonderful children and grandchildren, they are of course absolutely right but they are missing the essential point. Because that is exactly what you are now missing, the progress of your children, the blue eyes of your grandchildren, the touch of their smile.

I understood after beginning this letter to you that it did not make any sense at all only to express my sorrow. It was you who had suffered the greater loss and if I did not understand that, my loss would be nothing but sentimentality and self-pity. I must tell your tale, celebrate your life and times and see you through the fog of time. 'If only time could travel in reverse, would those days of my life that escaped my grasp return to me with the backward passing years.'[22]

I shall play our brief tape of life from the beginning to the end, reach across time to our first day together and seek the journey of your life in an arena of memories to find what you have been. I am rediscovering what I know I have lost.

Sarre, Dar es Salaam, Victoria, Bonn, Bremnes, Tokyo, Papeete, Harare, Copenhagen, Brussels, Oslo, Penrith, Oxford, Gatwick, Hythe, Exeter, Cwmbran, Newport, London and over fifty cities as flight attendant.

It is an outer and an inner journey.

THREE

✦

You did not just visit the world. You lived in eight countries and moved eleven times between 1966 and 2001. The first move was from England to Norway, then from Norway to Belgium, from Belgium to Denmark, from Denmark to England, from England to Norway, from Norway to Zimbabwe, from Zimbabwe to Japan, from Japan to Germany, from Germany to Norway, from Norway to Tanzania, from Tanzania to England. It is a tale of eleven homes in as many cities, packing and unpacking twenty-two times.

In spite of the hardship of moving and re-settling, you would resume life in each new city and home, always an optimistic, enthusiastic new beginning. Those who are outside the service and looking in, think it is an easy life. They see the privileges of travel and high society. The moves and constant uprooting were a heavy physical and emotional challenge.

It is true that 'nothing links these postings of ours, there is no continuity, it's like being reincarnated eight times in one life … you gradually build up a little world around yourself and then … you are suddenly sent off to the other side of the world to start all over again',[1] but your sense of adventure balanced the duty and hardship with excitement and discovery. My job was also your job, you made the same pledge to the service without any formal contractual obligation to do so but you accepted the challenge of diplomacy. Your loyalty is inscribed in numerous guest lists spanning four decades at 'Restaurant Residence Norway' in Brussels, Copenhagen, Harare, Tokyo, Bonn and Dar es Salaam.

As the camp follower, you had never come back to your own country to live until our retirement. At the end we would be back in the country where we met. Our search for a home took us finally to Old Road in the village of Sarre in Kent and a listed cottage from 1693 named Wychway after a wild elm in the garden. The cottage had a priest hole (a secret chamber and hiding place for a Roman Catholic priest in times of the Penal Laws[2]) and a wig cabinet. It had been an inn and a tea room visited by the pilots from Manston Airport during the Second World War. The house needed some renovation and we set about restoring one room at a time during our last posting to make it ready for a homecoming. 'Retirement comes inevitably at a stipulated time but with a sense of sadness rather than freedom. Why hurry home from a place where extraordinary days ... can happen ... it would be closing the door to adventure.'[3]

Retirement means that we lose our place in the world. As long as we were in the diplomatic play in a shared performance on the vagabond stage the final fall of the curtain seemed far away. You would not be long watching the seasonal change of the wild elm.

You had visited Sierra Leone as an air-hostess in the 1960s. In Freetown at the end of 2004, on a visit to Nina, we read together Graham Greene's novel *The Heart of the Matter* about the sympathetic, tormented and tragic Scobie, trapped between the despair of belief and the despair of unbelief. It would be my despair of disbelief that you would be dead only a month later. A God that took you away 'who was not human enough to love what he created'.[4]

'Are there no gods in heaven and earth? My dearest wife is dead!'[5]

I was suddenly there without you. 'Alone never felt more lonely than when you woke up and discovered you still had the house to yourself.'[6]

But I did not wish to make a new start without you in a different house from Wychway, to run away from the memories tied to the home. I do not see it as haunted by your absence; on the contrary, you are present in every room because you have been there and created the design for living in these same rooms. I know the rooms will sigh and not understand your absence as they search for your image.

FOUR

✦

But I must go back to the beginning. How did you and I meet? I had come to the new University of Exeter in the Summer Term of 1961 as a full time resident student.

Travelling was different then. It was a journey by ship from Oslo to Newcastle and then by train to Exeter.

I stayed one night in a pub in Exeter before I could sign on at my hall. In the pub I experienced traditional closing time for the first time as the publican at half past ten made known: 'Time, please, ladies and gentlemen, time.' A philosophical line on the art of irreplaceable time.

I got my room at Reed Hall which I shared with one student from Germany and one from Sierra Leone.

The English Department and its key lecturer and tutor, K.W. Salter, received overseas students with enthusiasm and opened treasures of English Literature. He would sometimes pause in his lecture and emphasize: 'I suggest to you that this is a fine line.'

Towards the end of term a student contact between Barton Place and Reed Hall led to this invitation:

> The Warden, House Manager,
> President and members of Barton Place
> request the pleasure of the company of
> Mr. Nils-Johan Jørgensen
> at
> A Summer Ball
> on Tuesday, 27ᵗʰ June, 1961
> 8 p.m. – 2 a.m.
>
> Formal Dress   R.S.V.P.
> Reception 8 – 8.30p.m.   The Social Secretary

I met you. 'In the three seconds you have to look at her, you actually fall in love, and in those moments, you can actually know the taste of her kiss, the feel of her skin against yours, the sound of her laugh, how she'll look at you and make you whole.'[1]

It is not enough to say you were stunning and I do not mean just beautiful, bright and elegant. I sensed the courage of your soul, the dream to cross borders and to explore the wider world. I commented on your hands. Your hand holding mine had beauty and strength. 'Tennis and riding,' you smiled. Your hands would never fail and never let go as we crossed the mountains and the plains together. 'So it is plain that in her greeting resided all my joy.'[2]

You wore a perfect light blue dress. I had found the blue flower.[3] The love I had been searching and longing for.

Vera Lloyd, who was the lecturer in English phonetics and drama, gave me the part of Bassanio in an open-air production of *The Merchant of Venice* in front of Reed Hall. In the tenth century romantic story *Taketori Monogatari*[4] tests are set for the suitors to win the beautiful Kaguya-hime and in the *Merchant of Venice* Portia has to introduce tests for her admirers.

What tests would you set for me and would I pass?

The next day you came to see the first performance of the play. I spotted you from the stage as you came up the road in a black dress with blue stripes.

I had promised to take another girl to a dance that same evening but I did not wish to do this after I had met you. I made an irreverent excuse. The girl was not amused.

So had I passed the first test by declining all others and created a fine line?

We met again and the sweet winds did gently kiss the trees. The first kiss. Yes, there was a time between the first and the last kiss but the time in between was not long enough.

The term was too soon at an end; you had to leave for home in Monmouthshire and I had to leave for Norway. As I walked with you up Wrefords Lane to Barton Place I felt that I must see you again. 'I'll find you one day,' I said. I had a strange sense of predestination.

I sent you a card which I cryptically ended *a.m.l.* (All my love). Later that summer in Oslo I received the first letter from you. It was a letter full of news and details, the way you always would write. You told me about your family and your home and the freedom of taking your father's car for a run. It was an invitation to keep in touch.

On the basis of my studies and references from Exeter I applied for the Norwegian scholarship at Wadham College, Oxford. The English Department of the University of Oslo gave the application support and to my delight and surprise I was selected by the Academic Council. I packed my bag, sailed from Oslo to Newcastle and took the train to Oxford.

Did anyone mention fate, inevitable destiny? Would you and I have met again if I had not come to Oxford? What *kami* steered me towards an application in the first place? The three goddesses of fate, Clotho, Lachesis and Atropos, birth, life and death, had crossed our path. I met you again. Life began and death seemed far away. The beginning was as bright and hopeful, as the end was sudden, dark and cruel.

The 350th anniversary of Wadham College was celebrated with a commemoration ball in July 1963. A steel band played in the

J.C.R. quadrangle. A cabaret was provided by the ubiquitous David Frost. We danced to the music of Johnny Dankworth and Humphrey Lyttelton. *The Tatler* covered the event with a picture of us together and the headline 'Night to remember' in the 17 July issue. And there we are, or there we were, sitting out in the Wadham Hall.

'Once there had been a tinted photograph of his wife on the wall but he had taken it down because it made him too lonely to see it …'⁵

I sometimes look at the images of our life together preserved in the albums you made. Yes, that makes me lonely.

Time.

FIVE

✦

When my time at Oxford had ended we parted in London on 2 December 1962.

You made this entry in your diary: 'Saw Darling off at 9.20. Train home at 12.55. Snowing. Train Full. Home 5.45. Miserable Jill.'

On my way back by train and ship via Hook of Holland and Copenhagen I sent you a card: 'I think of the future to master the misery I feel now. Easter will soon come, spring and summer; in the meantime we shall just prepare our life.'

I found that you always carried that card in your handbag, folded over and tucked away with the patina of age.

In a folder I found your little scrap-book from our first journey together, a flight with British United Airways from London to Barcelona, organized by the National Union of Students in the Summer of 1962.

You had carefully preserved the ticket coupons, our hotel and restaurant receipts etc. from our island hopping as we sailed first to Menorca, flew to Majorca, sailed to Ibiza and then to Valencia. We went to museums, bullfights and night-clubs. We found secluded beaches in Menorca. We used up the little money we had and I had to make a speedy transfer from my humble account.

Sailing between Ibiza and Valencia at night, a group of the Spanish passengers sang 'Ave Maria' under a full moon. It stayed with us, at our wedding and at the memorial service for you. Between the first and the last 'Ave Maria' we would visit many islands and many cities:

> As you set out for Ithaka
> Hope the voyage is a long one,
> full of adventure, full of discovery ...[1]

Good fortune is not guaranteed but take a chance on life and marvellous journeys may happen. There will be pleasure, joy and rare excitement along the way.

Our first journey together held a promise of a future full of adventure and discovery.

The journey itself is the key. The promise was honoured.

SIX

✦

A nd so you reached for the sky. You wore a uniform consisting
of a navy blue pencil skirt and jacket and a delicate white
blouse. The jacket had four buttons in front and an embroidered
golden wing on the left. Your amazing, long chestnut hair was
elevated in perfect style under a small circular hat. The hat carried a
round embroidered badge with the airline logo on the left side.
With promotion came the golden rings on the jacket sleeves. The
shoes were also in navy with high stiletto heels.

It was an elegant, conservative uniform in navy and gold.

You were employed by British United Airways (BUA) as an air-
hostess from 22 April 1963 until 22 October 1966. BUA was the
largest independent British based airline in the 1960s with Sir
Freddie Laker from Canterbury as managing director from 1961.
During your time with BUA you trained and flew on the Bristol,
Carvair, Britannia, Viscount, BAC 1-11 and VC 10, on routes to
Europe, the Middle East, Africa and South America. You were
promoted to the position of number one hostess on 1 May 1966.

☐

Ellen Church, a registered nurse and a qualified pilot, was the first to suggest the recruitment of air-hostesses. She was employed by Boeing Air Transport as the world's first female flight attendant to head the selection and training of candidates for the emerging aviation adventure.

Until then only stewards had been employed on the German Zeppelins, on the US carriers Stout Airways, Western Airways and Pan American World Airways and on British Imperial Airways.

Ellen Church introduced a demanding standard, providing not only elegance and glamour, but more importantly the ability to keep calm in an emergency. The key responsibility was passenger safety. A new and exciting profession in aviation took off as Ellen Church welcomed eleven passengers onboard a flight from Oakland Airport, California, 15 May 1930.

☐

You came to visit me in Oslo at the Student Town in April 1963 before your first employment with BUA at Lydd and again in November. You matriculated at the University of Oslo on 18 November and completed your first intensive course in Norwegian (and obtained A).

In the early 1960s joining an airline was a way of getting out to the wider world. You had your grandfather's wanderlust and the geographical knowledge to make your journeys part of an enthusiastic exploration.

Your flying days would take you to over fifty destinations on regular flights, tour holidays and troop transport: internal flights to Edinburgh, Glasgow and Manchester, continental European routes to Amsterdam, Akrotiri, Athens, Barcelona, Bardufoss, Basel, Belfast, Berlin, Bucharest, Deauville, Dubrovnik, Düsseldorf, Faro, Geneva, Genoa, Gibraltar, Guernsey, Gütersloh, Hannover, Ibiza, Jersey, Le Touquet, Liège, Ljubljana, Lourdes, Malaga, Malta, Naples, Nice, Ostend, Palma, Pérpignan, Rijswijk, Rimini, Rome, Rotterdam, Seville, Strasbourg, Valencia, Venice, Verona, Wildenroth, Zürich and international routes to Aden, Bahrain,

Entebbe, Freetown, Lagos, Las Palmas, Nairobi, Rio, Salisbury, Tenerife and Tripoli.

The design of your first aircraft, the Bristol Freighter, was created by Wing Commander 'Taffy' Powell by adapting the design of the Bristol Bombay Bomber to fly passengers with their cars from Britain to continental Europe. The first model was introduced in 1948 and the British United Air Ferries (BUAF) service was opened at Lydd Ferryfield airport in Kent in 1961. The larger Carvair (Car-via-air) was a converted DC-4 to carry twenty-five passengers and five cars. The major modifications were a new, lengthened nose section and a cargo door allowing nose loading for cars and an elevated flight deck, in fact very similar to the later design of the Boeing 747. It entered into service with BUAF in 1962.

The BUAF Bristol and Carvair service from Lydd was very popular and a great success for BUA at a time before the introduction of hovercraft, hydrofoils and faster channel ferries.

The Carvair was given a glamorous supporting role in the third James Bond film in 1964, based on Ian Fleming's novel, *Goldfinger*. The German actor, Gert Fröbe, playing the super villain Auric Goldfinger, travelled with his vintage, gold Rolls Royce (registration AU 1) on British United flight BF 400 to Geneva. We see the car being loaded onboard the aircraft and Goldfinger embarking. James Bond watches from the airport car park in his Aston Martin and continues on the next flight to Geneva. Thus an image of the Carvair, BUAF and Lydd airport of 1964 have been preserved in this vintage Bond film.

You drove a green Mini. The car was invented in 1959 and became the design classic of the 1960s.

You transferred to Gatwick in 1964, first to the long-range Bristol Britannia and then to the medium-range Vickers Viscount. Both aircraft stand out as the finest turboprop designs ever in service.

After your initiation on these four propeller aircraft, the jet-age arrived and you were soon trained on the short range BAC (British Aircraft Corporation) 1-11 that replaced the Viscount. It was also the second short-haul jet aircraft to enter service after the French Caravelle.

The prize was the beautiful, long distance, four engine VC 10, the British jet designed and developed by Vickers-Armstrong which first flew in 1962 and was operated by BUA from 1964. This is perhaps the most elegant jet passenger airliner ever designed, the swan of the skies, technical and artistic.

□

Looking back forty years later, your time with BUA is a fly-past of unique British aircraft and aviation history. All six types of aircraft are now inside or near the door of a museum. Like the stonefly, the damselfly, the dragon-fly and the mayfly they would flaunt their wings and cruise for a day only (*ephēmeros*). They are the symbols of the excellence of the British aircraft industry.

I have seen them all taking off with you onboard from Lydd and Gatwick. As they speed down the runway of my memory, I remember you and the golden wing on your jacket.

I continued at Oslo University. We met as often as we could in Norway or in England. The ties that bind. Letters crossing oceans.

After your years of flying we had planned to come to Oxford. You had been accepted by St. Hugh's College and I would continue at Linacre where I had come at the beginning of 1966 after completing my studies in Oslo.

Then a diplomatic career was offered.

SEVEN

✦

With this ring I thee wed. On 19 November 1966, I placed a gold ring on the fourth finger of your left hand.

Levinus Lemnius writes, in *The Secret Miracles of Nature* (1571), that an artery runs down to the fourth finger of the left hand. The gold ring is placed upon that finger to convey the beneficial influence of gold to the heart. The tradition of wearing the gold wedding ring upon this finger is associated with the Renaissance ranking of gold as the primate of metals, the terrestrial substance containing the perfect mixture of the four elements, free from rust and decay.

The wedding reception was held at the Priory Country Club in Carleon. *The South Wales Argus* had interviewed you before the wedding under the headline 'Marriage only temporarily "grounds" air hostess Jill':

Air-hostesses find themselves grounded when they marry. But not Jill Borlase, daughter of Colonel and Mrs Borlase of Olway Close, Llanyravon, Cwmbran. True she has given up her job as British United Airways senior air stewardess, but her marriage to Nils-Johan Jørgensen, holds the prospect of much travel and the chance to live in practically any part of the world for Mr Jørgensen is First Secretary in the Royal Norwegian Ministry of Foreign Affairs.

For her wedding at All Saints Church, Llanfrechfa, Miss Borlase wore a full-length sheath-lined gown of white duchesse satin with long train falling from the shoulders. The sleeves and train were edged with gulpure lace and she carried a small spray of white rosebuds attached to her prayer book.

Three of her cousins, Joyce Elizabeth Muir, Angela and Corin Boyd were bridesmaids and they wore long sheath line dresses in deep kingfisher blue. They carried sprays of pink carnations and white freesias.

There would be more flights.

EIGHT

✦

Soon after arrival in Oslo you made contact with the Open University and were invited to teach English classes at various levels, including phonetics courses. You joined the programme introduced by the Royal Society for the Encouragement of Arts, Manufactures and Commerce and obtained a Certificate in the Teaching of English as a Second or Foreign Language.

Phonetics became your target topic and specialization. You were first recruited as a speaker in an extensive recording project, language laboratory drills for pronunciation and listening practice based on Michael Walton's books. This was followed by the recording of various other language teaching texts, including phonetics and pronunciation practice material at the University of Oslo for the British Institute based on *English Pronunciation for Scandinavians* by J. Windsor Lewis. You made a series of English language programmes for the School Radio Department at the Norwegian Broadcasting Corporation. You also recorded a language film for Bergen Bank.

You were then offered a lectureship in English in the Department of Modern Languages at the Norwegian School of Management (B.I.), teaching phonetics, grammar, literature, commercial correspondence, translation and English and American institutions in both lectures and groups to students in the field of tertiary education.

□

Your literature course at B.I. included Shaw's *Pygmalion*. The last musical we watched together in London was *My Fair Lady.* If only the goddess Venus could bring you back to life like Pygmalion's ivory statue.[1] But no prayer can do that.

NINE

✦

We were expecting our first child in Oslo in April 1971. You were told that the unborn child had not turned and it would be a breech delivery. As we waited for the signs of the impending birth we walked together to the harbour in Oslo and watched the sailing ship, *Christian Radich*. The news of a breech birth made you cry as we watched the silent rocking of the ship and the masts connecting with the spring sky. In those days it would be a natural birth; today it is a caesarian in the same circumstances. Soon the waiting was over and we drove together to Aker Hospital as the clock ticked towards the beginning of a new life.

I was allowed to dress in white and sit with you in the room until the final stages of the birth when rules demanded that I had to leave. The dramatic process was soon successfully over and a little girl with open eyes greeted us and the world for the first time at 4.30 a.m. Tears of joy. In your little red pocket diary for Saturday 17 April 1971 you wrote: 'The greatest night in my life. LISA.'

Maurice, in the film *Venus*, invites Jessie to the National Gallery to view the nude portrait by Diego Velázquez. Maurice tells Jessie: 'For most men a woman's naked body is the most beautiful thing they will ever see.' Jessie asks: 'What is the most beautiful thing a girl sees?' Maurice answers: 'Her first child.'

Your line confirms Maurice's second line. As for me I can confirm his first line. Your naked body was the most beautiful.

TEN

✦

We set out together by ship from Kristiansand to Amsterdam and continued to our Embassy and mission to the EC in Brussels in 1972 as the final preparations for Norwegian membership heated up. We moved into Park Hotel with our new-born Lisa before we could take possession of our new home, an apartment in Residence Trianon in Avenue d'Huart.

The Capital of Europe. Grand Place, perhaps the most beautiful square in the world, surrounded by the tower of the town hall and the merchant palaces.

You would go riding among the beech trees in Forest de Soignés and on a rare occasion we would have dinner at *La Villa Lorraine* (and drink wine from 1966), the only Belgian restaurant at the time granted three rosettes by Michelin. Madame Pierre Harmel, the Belgian Foreign Minister's wife, invited the spouses who had arrived in Brussels after 17 February that year to a Reception in Prieuré de Val Duchesse. We went to the Opera National and the Theatre de la Monnaie.

I represented the Embassy to report from a session of the European Parliament, Maison de l'Europe, in Strasbourg. You and Lisa (just over one year old) joined me and we drove past landscapes and trenches from the First World War and visited the family you had stayed with when you were at school. We stayed at Hotel du Parc in Obernai, Strasbourg.

During the interim period after the EC negotiations were over, we waited for the September referendum in Norway. The free trade agreements between the enlarged Community, the six members of the EC together with the four new countries scheduled to join (Britain, Ireland, Denmark and Norway), and the EFTA non-candidates (Iceland, Finland, Sweden, Switzerland, Austria and Portugal) were signed in Brussels on 22 July 1972, six months after Norway had signed the Accession Treaty. Foreign Minister Andreas Cappelen came to the ceremony in Palais d'Egmont and signed for Norway as a prospective member.

We drove to the small town Les Lecques in Saint-Cyr-Sur-Mer, in the south south of France for a short holiday as the people of Norway geared up for the EC vote.

□

The backache started in the evening of 5 July 1973. At 20.15 you called your doctor, the gynaecologist J.H. Blackman. We set out in the car and arrived at Edith Cavell at 21.30. It was a very hot evening. The doctor arrived at 21.50. You began pushing at 21.56 and pushed for 25 minutes. Nina was born at 22.50. I was beside you throughout the birth. I spoke to Nina. She seemed to listen.

When you were still at Edith Cavell I had to tell you that we had been posted to Copenhagen because of replanning of staff after the Norwegian referendum. We had hoped to stay on in Brussels a bit longer. The 'no' at the vote was a 'no' to the continuation of our posting in Brussels.

Nina would start a journey, not just with us to all our postings, but would then continue a career in international law from Oxford to the international criminal tribunals in The Hague, Arusha, Freetown and Phnom Penh.

□

The Norwegian 'No' in the referendum of 25 September was a bleak day for all those who believed in Norway's place in Europe. Britain and Norway parted company. An historic chance for Norway was missed. Norway then signed a trade agreement with the EC on 14 May 1973. Five of the EFTA non-candidates of 1972 would become members of the EU while Norway remained outside the club after new negotiations and a referendum in 1994.

ELEVEN

✦

I was invited to look over Danish shoulders into the EC – a gesture from the Danish Government after the result of the referendum. Norway had become the Outside Country and any remedy to follow the development of European integration was seen as most welcome.

We settled into our new home in Hjortekær at Lyngby and Lisa attended the local kindergarten. Not yet three years old and three countries already.

You found a nearby riding school and went riding in Dyrehaven.

We had two official visits during our time in Denmark: King Olav V in 1974 and the Prime Minister, Trygve Bratteli, in 1975.

As a *Nacht und Nebel* political prisoner in Germany between 1942 and 1945 Bratteli was moved between seven different concentration camps, including Sachenhausen and Dachau. He was rescued in 1945.

You and I often reflected upon how remarkable it was that he would become a convinced spokesman for European integration and for Norway's full participation. Europe must never again be brought to the deepest circle of evil, which nearly destroyed its civilization and the essence of democracy. He was your political hero.

King Olav V of Norway was known as *Folkekongen* (The People's King). He had stood tall together with his father, King Haakon VII, as Germany invaded Norway and they continued the fight against occupation and oppression as symbols of freedom from exile in England. The King's mother, Queen Maud of Norway, was the daughter of Edward VII.

We became part of an intensive royal programme and you had the honour of being introduced to the King of Norway and the Queen of Denmark.

The comedy *Kierlighed uden Strømper* (Love without stockings) by the Norwegian playwright Johan Herman Wessel, who studied and settled in Denmark, had been chosen for the gala performance at the Royal Theatre, thus ending a successful visit with a smile.

TWELVE

✦

We sailed north of the north wind. In 1977 we became the owners of a Marieholm sailing-boat. I named her *Rogerlinde* in your honour after the first Duchess of Taillefer in Angoulême.

... to cleave that sea in the gentle autumnal season, murmuring the name of each islet, is to my mind the joy most apt to transport the heart of man into paradise. Nowhere else can one pass so easily and serenely from reality to dreams.[1]

Indre Elgsnes in Northern Norway was once a thriving society with continuous settlement dating back to the Bronze Age maintained by the riches of the sea. It became a trading place in the seventeenth century, with a primary school, court sessions and accommodation for travellers. A place where 'generations have trod, have trod, have trod ... bleared, smeared with toil'.[2] I was one-month-old when my parents moved there to live for the next two years. The settlement policies of the 1950s signalled the end of the village. Only the houses remain.

You came ashore for the first time one sunny spring day in May when Lisa was one year old. We went there with my parents in their open wooden boat, Lisa in her pram in the middle of the boat. We aimed for the old boat landing and continued to my grandfather's house. We sat down outside. An abandoned place maintained by the beauty of the sea, the islands and the mountains.

There would be many summer mornings when you would come back. Lisa and Nina would play on the beach and find crabs and shells. What you will never see is Lily, Bear and Pani now playing on that beach and finding the same toys from the sea with shrieks of excitement as they splash into the clear water.

And now when I am out at sea without you with the silence of the sails I think of days when we hoisted the spinnaker together. I paraphrase the poet: 'Jeg tenker på dager som denne du ikke fikk lov til å leve' (I think of days like these when you were not allowed to live).

I anchored at Indre Elgsnes and I took in the view we knew so well – the mountain Elgen, the sandy beach and the old homestead. It was one of these rare days when everything came together, the sea the sun and the wind. On such a day you would say, 'this is sailing'. I wished you could still hear the wind. An eagle making a wide circle seemed to look out for you.

Suddenly and imperceptibly fog filled the air and hid the mountains and the sea. Where are you?

THIRTEEN

✦

During the home posting in Oslo between Copenhagen and Harare, you entered into a new career when you were employed as a member of the editorial staff of the Norwegian Press Agency, *Norinform*, which issued news items and feature articles about Norway in foreign languages.

You were promoted to be Editor of both the daily 'Norway News Bulletin' and the weekly 'Norinform' issues in English. This strengthened your knowledge of the Norwegian language and of Norwegian politics and current affairs. The Head of the Press Department in the Ministry of Foreign Affairs, Director General Bjørn Jensen, gave you a *summa cum laude* written reference for your outstanding efforts – 'pleasant, active and effective'.

You were approached by *The Times* (London) and became the correspondent (stringer) in Norway. You held another position in the educational field as lecturer in phonetics at Sagene College of Education before our posting to Salisbury (Harare).

FOURTEEN

✦

You were the Senior Hostess on the last British United VC 10 out of Salisbury before Ian Smith announced Unilateral Declaration of Independence (UDI) on 11 November 1965. Rhodesia became a closed and isolated country from the international community until independence on 18 April 1980.

We left in the evening of 4 February 1981 to open the first Norwegian Embassy in Salisbury. After a stop-over in Nairobi we continued south in cloudless sunshine and we soon had a splendid view of the snows of Kilimanjaro. The British Airways Captain summed up the mood succinctly: 'She looks very beautiful this morning.' I looked at you and nodded: 'Yes, you do.' You smiled,

Rhodesia was an undiscovered country for Norway before 1980 and it was an unknown part of the world for most Norwegians before UDI in 1965. The Norwegian community was very small and there had been very little feedback from family and personal contacts between Norway and Rhodesia, minimal trade and no political contact. The fight for freedom and independence put Rhodesia on the map. Norwegian voluntary organizations began to support the struggle and humanitarian assistance was granted to the Patriotic Front after 1974. In 1980 the Foreign Secretary, Knut Frydenlund, decided to open a Norwegian Embassy.

I used to cycle between our flat in Oslo and the Foreign Ministry during the four seasons in all weathers. Before Christmas in 1980 I was appointed First Secretary (and Chargé d'Affaires a.i.) at our new Embassy in Salisbury and speeding home I got a puncture. You used to tell me that I said: 'I had a puncture – by the way, we are going to Salisbury.'

I thus became the first Norwegian diplomatic representative in Salisbury (renamed Harare). I know you looked forward to this posting. We came together, you, Lisa, Nina and I, to sunshine and summer in our winter clothes and moved into Monomotapa Hotel, room 707. This room was to be the first chancery of the Embassy and our home for more than three months. A new office building had to be found and residences had to be restored. I found a suitable building on the corner of Second Street and Montague Avenue and we moved into our house in Borrowdale. Lisa and Nina started at the local Chisipite Junior School.

We shared the optimism of the country and I participated as a delegate to the very successful 'Zimbabwe conference on reconstruction and development (Zimcord)' in March 1981. The first Norwegian development programme was introduced for rural water development. Ominously, in view of what has happened during Mugabe's sunset years, his Planning Minister, Chidzero, stated and repeated at the conference: 'Without a successful land distribution programme this society cannot hold together.'

The land distribution agenda fell into disrepute and twenty years later the pearl of Africa had become a failed state without agricultural export.

In 1981 we believed in Zimbabwe as a model African country that was going to build a successful economic model in a socialist, one party system. The British economist Roger Riddell, at Mugabe's request, produced a report on resettlement and land distribution in June 1981. Reconciliation was the watchword and Mugabe promised possibilities for everyone and a tolerant society.

International society supported the wind of change and openness and contact with the outside world after isolation. Mugabe was invited to Norway in September 1981, the Foreign Relations Committee of the *Storting* (Parliament) visited Zimbawe at the beginning of 1983 and in 1984 Crown Princess Sonja as the representative of the Norwegian Red Cross, together with the Norwegian Refugee Council visited Zimbawe.

Zimbabwe was then an attractive tourist destination and Victoria Falls, *Mosi-ou-tunya* (the smoke that thunders), was rediscovered.

There was a sense of discovery and adventure in coming to a land that had effectively been cut off from the world for a very long time. As an Embassy we had to begin from scratch and build the infrastructure and systems required. In a wave of enthusiasm which seemed to reflect the mood of the country you created a home and an environment that our children to this day consider the perfect childhood.

As a child and teenager in Monmouthshire you had learned to ride and had taken part in show jumping and cross-country events. You connected with the sport when you had the opportunity in Brussels and Copenhagen but it was in Harare that you again had the chance to ride and share in Lisa and Nina's progress in show jumping.

In Tokyo you prepared a photo album from our time in Zimbawe. On the last page you have written: 'And so we had to turn our backs on Harare and 16 Breach Road – time heals all the pain?' You loved our time there. It was *eutopia* – a good place (then).

What gradually happened in Zimbabwe in recent years we would only observe with total, sorrowful disbelief. It would have amazed you that forty-two years after UDI was declared, British Airways flew out of Harare for the last time on 28 October 2007. Several international carriers had resumed their services to Harare after independence in 1980 and they continued flights until passenger numbers began to decline sharply as a result of the disposession of white farmers in 2000, the decline in tourism and the economy spinning out of control. BA was the last to leave, a further blow to tourism. Imperial Airways had started flights to Salisbury in 1932 and also introduced landing and a flying boat jetty on the Zambezi River. The jetty is still there. One day BA and other international airlines will again have services to Harare and to the wonder of *Mosi-ou-tunya*.

FIFTEEN

✦

You used to say that to come to Japan was to come abroad - to a new language, a new culture and new customs, an esoteric world.

We arrived in Nihon (the source of the sun) in 1984 into a third time zone with SAS SK 989 which took us past Svalbard, the North Pole and a scheduled stop in Anchorage before we continued across the Indian Ocean. The Cold War was still a reality and civil aviation had to avoid Soviet air space. I had been appointed Counsellor at the Embassy in Tokyo on 15 June 1984 and was given rank as Minister Counsellor a year later.

You would touch and be influenced by this unique culture. We were invited by the Music Department of the Imperial Household to attend a programme of Gagaku (meaning elegant music), the ancient form of Japanese music and the oldest form of musical culture in the world. We watched the Kabuki play *Daikyoji Mukashi Gyomi* (Osan and Mohei), first performed in 1715 and a performance of *Bunraku*.[1] We were invited by the Ministry of Foreign Affairs and the Japan Sumo Association to attend a Sumo tournament. We went for Bonsai viewing in Omiya (grand shrine), Saitama Prefecture, to Hiroshima and Nagasaki, including the

47

shipyard of Mitsubishi and the island of Deshima, to Kobe, Kyoto and Nara.

On an outing to the Imperial stock farm in Tochigi Prefecture we watched *Horo-Hiki* (flowing streamer on horseback), a form of equitation dating from the Edo period and performed by a pair of horsemen in traditional ceremonial costume, releasing a ten metres long silk streamer horizontally as the horses gather speed. Afterwards, you were invited to ride one of the horses.

We attended the celebration of the Birthday of His Majesty the Emperor at Iikura House and His Majesty's Garden Party at the Akasaka Imperial Gardens. You joined the Norway-Japan Society, the Foreign Service Training Institute, the College Women's Association of Japan and the Japanese group six of the Elizabeth Kai. You were interviewed on the NHK Radio English Conversation programme. You studied *ikebana* and *sumie* (wash painting).

From Tokyo we visited Saipan, Guam, Hong Kong, Seoul, Panmunjom and Bali.

We represented Norway at the Heads of Mission audience with the Emperor on his 84th birthday and you were dressed in the *Nordlandsbunad*, the national dress for Northern Norway, created and given to you by your mother-in-law. In a letter to your parents you gave the following account of the event:

We left in state in the official car, flag flying. Imperial guards and police were on the long drive. I felt suitably dressed in my bunad as the cars reached the main door. The guests were graciously ushered into the reception room until we were called in order of precedence to proceed to the receiving room. Then the Imperial family came in and stood while the Dean of the Diplomatic Corps expressed our congratulations. The Emperor said a few words and we were called to the line and presented. It was interesting especially when the Crown Princess held me back so long talking about my costume that I felt I was delaying the proceedings. I wished her a pleasant time in Norway in June on their official visit. They were all there including the Prince who is studying in Oxford so by the time I reached the end of the line the champagne prize was more than welcome. When members of the Royal Family came to join the guests, Prince Tomohito of Mikasa, Crown Prince Akihito's first cousin (who is President of the Norway/Japan Society) spoke to Nils-Johan first. Then Princess Nobuko of Mikasa came to speak to me – I was standing with the West German and the Australian representatives – and I politely asked after her two small children and she complained that they were always catching something just having begun in kindergarten. I think my two other companions were rather impressed with our casual conversation but then we had met before at a dinner at our Embassy.

Fiction in the form of letters, the epistolary novels, first appeared in the Restoration period, cf. Aphra Behn's novel *Oroonoko* (1688). Samuel Richardson incorporated the epistolary method in his novels (*Pamela* and *Clarissa*) and letters would fulfil a purpose similar to the soliloquy in a play and the stream of consciousness in later novels.

You were a most generous epistolarian in a time before fax and e-mail. During three decades you would write hundreds of inspired letters with your school Parker pen reflecting the changes and challenges of diplomatic life. You observed and shared your private and immediate experience of life with distant but ever present roots.

I have found and kept the letters, the soliloquies, the streams of consciousness. As e-mail and text messaging take over they are a reminder of a time now past. Beautiful handwriting from a beautiful hand. 'Mit deiner Hand ergriff mich ein Vertrauen, das sicher mich durch alle Stürme trägt' (With your hand moved a trust that carry me safely through all storms).[2]

The hand that first touched mine in Exeter.

SIXTEEN

✦

In 1987, we circumnavigated the globe: Tokyo – Honolulu – Papeete – Los Angeles – Amsterdam – Evenes – London – Anchorage – Tokyo. The main goal was French Polynesia and Tahiti. We arrived on UTA flight 552 'and there, on the ideal reef, thunders the everlasting sea'[1] around one hundred and thirty reef-fringed islands. The Garden of Eden.

We were received by the friendly and generous Norwegian honorary consul, Victor Wan Fa Siu and his family. He could relate that I was the first representative from the Norwegian Foreign Ministry that had visited the islands in his time as Consul.

We stayed on the island of Mo'orea. At Hotel Sofitel Tiare we had a splendid over-water thatched roof bungalow decorated in traditional style. The French Manager told us that an American guest staying at a similar bungalow had complained that the sea disturbed him so much that he could not sleep and demanded a different room on land: 'I give them paradise, and they don't want it', concluded the Manager.

We were quite content with paradise.

SEVENTEEN

✦

In your pocket diary from 1987 I found the following lines:

All went according to plan until a shadow was cast from a phone call from Penrith to Harstad on the weekend of 16 August. On Friday 14 August they had called for a doctor on emergency duty to attend to Daddy who was diagnosed with water on the lung. On Friday 21 August Lisa and I arrived to find a very changed grandfather. Nevertheless, courage prevailed until after the departure of Nils-Johan and Nina on 3 September and his determination continued until the day Lisa and I left for school on 8 September. After that he could do nothing but succumb to the pain. Did he realize these were the final farewells?

You continued to stay with your father and took him for a last drive around his beloved Ullswater and spent the last night with him on 30 September before you went back to Tokyo. 'Final goodnight to Daddy. This will be the end and I know it. How long will he last?'

You were so close. He had always taken an interest in your development and progress and you relied on his calm and considered advice. He had tears in his eyes whenever you two parted. I could see that.

We were often so far away from our parents.

A phone call in October informed you that your father had died. So you left again to prepare for the funeral. Your mother seemed lost and helpless. You wrote the day before the funeral: 'Will Daddy and Nils-Johan be proud of me tomorrow?' It was always so easy to be proud of you. Now started the difficult process of looking after your mother from Tokyo.

Four days later the worst gales since records began hit London and the south-east. Kew Gardens were wrecked. There was flooding in Cumbria. Three days later came the international financial crash. It was as if nature and society echoed your darkest hour. On 5 November you flew back to Tokyo.

Your father, a civil engineer, distinguished himself in the Second World War, first at Dunkirk between 1939 and 1940. We have perhaps forgotten the hardship of the campaign, the extreme cold winter, how brutal and devastating the withdrawal was and the terror of the evacuation.

After Dunkirk he commanded a Bomb Disposal Unit in London (a lethal task) from 1940 to 1941, before serving in Military Intelligence at the War Office from 1942 to 1943. He was promoted to the rank of Colonel in 1943 (having started as a Lieutenant in 1939), transferred to 21 Army Group and served in France and Germany after the Normandy landings.

You were born as the bombs fell over London.

After the war he was appointed the first Chief Engineer of the Cwmbran Development Corporation in 1953 and he was instrumental in the planning and development of Cwmbran new town in Monmothshire. He served as a member of Council of the Institute of Civil Engineers. In retirement your parents went back to their roots in the Lake District.

We were the lucky few who had known your father. 'We should never forget they made great sacrifices so that our lives could be a lot more comfortable today.'[1]

You, Nina and I visited Dunkirk and Normandy in honour of your father's dedication and service to his country.

EIGHTEEN

✦

'Let my girl's name stream on through a thousand ages.'[1]

I know you were proud of your ancestry and curious to know more. Let me go back with you through the mist of time to Angoulême and Cornwall to seek your roots in medieval history.

The German Romantic poet, a student of medieval history and literature, professor and politician, Johann Ludwig Uhland (1787–1862), wrote this eulogistic ballad about the legendary Taillefer:

Normannenherzog Wilhelm sprach einmal:
'Wer singet in meinem Hof und in meinem Saal?
Wer singet von Morgen bis in die späte Nacht
So lieblich, das mir das Herz im Leibe lacht?'
(Norman Duke William once aloud did call:
'Who singeth in my court and in my hall?
Who singeth so witchingly, from morn to night,
And makes my heart leap up in sheer delight?')
    'Das is der Taillefer, der so gerne singt,
Im Hofe, wann er das Rad am Brunnen schwingt,
Im Saale, wann er das Feuer schüret und facht,
Wann er abends sich legt, und wann er morgens erwacht.'

('It is Taillefer, as he is free to tell,
Who sings in the court when he is at the well, –
Who sings in the hall when he fans the faggot-flame,
At break of morn, and at fall of eve the same.')

    Der Herzog sprach: 'Ich hab' einen guten Knecht,
Den Taillefer, der dienet mir fromm und recht;
Er treibt mein Rad und schüret mein Feuer gut
Und singet so hell, das hohet mir den Mut.'
(Then quoth the Duke, 'I have a groom right true,
Taillefer, – he serveth me with honour due;
He draws me water and fans my fire aright,
And sings so loud, that it nerves my arm with might.')

    Da sprach der Taillefer: 'Und war' ich frei,
Viel besser wollt' ich dienen und singen dabei.
Wie wollt' ich dienen dem Herzog hoch zu Pferd!
Wie wollt' ich singen und klingen mit Schild und Schwert!'
(Quoth Taillefer, 'and sooth, if I were free,
Far better, my lord would I serve and sing to thee.
How would I serve my Duke on a charger high!
Would sing and ring with shield sword thereby.')

    Nicht lange, so ritt der Taillefer ins Gefield
Auf einem hohen Pferde mit Schwert und mit Schild.
Des Herzogs Schwester schaute von Turm ins Feld;
Sie sprach: 'Dort reitet, bei Gott, ein stattlicher Held.'
(Not long was it ere Taillefer rode afield
Upon a charger tall, with sword and shield.
Duke William's sister gaz'd from the turret high,
Quoth she – 'by heavens! A stately knight rides by.')

    Und als er ritt vorüber an Fräuleins Turm,
Da sang er bald wie ein Lüftlein, bald wie ein Sturm.
Sie sprach: 'Der singet, das ist eine herrliche Lust;
Es zittert der Turm, und es zittert mein Herz in der Brust!'
(As he rode past where stood that sweet lady-form,
He sang like the light breeze, and now he sang like the storm.
'Such lovely sounds', quoth she, 'I never yet knew!
The tower doth quiver, my bosom is quivering too.'

Der Herzog Wilhelm fuhr wohl über das Meer,
Er fuhr nach Engelland mit gewaltigen Heer.
Er sprang vom Schiffe, da fiel er auf die Hand;
'Hei', rief er, ich fass' und ergreife dich, Engelland!'
(Norman Duke William sail'd across the sea;
To England with a mighty host steer'd he;
Then he leap'd ashore and fell upon his hand,
'Ha!' cried he, 'I clutch and seize on thee England.')
    Als nun das Normannenheer zum Sturme schritt,
Der edle Taillefer vor dem Herzog ritt:
'Manch Jährlein hab' ich gesungen und Feuer geschürt,
Manch Jährlein gesungen und Schwert und Lanze geführt.
(When now the Normans to the battle strode,
The noble Taillefer 'fore Duke William rode:
'Full many a year have I sung and fed the brand,
Full many a year have I sung with sword in hand.')
    Und hab' ich euch gedient und gesungen zu Dank,
Zuerst als ein Knecht und dann als ein Ritter frank,
So lasst mich das entgelten am heutigen Tag!
Vergönnet mir auf die Feinde den ersten Schlag!'
(And if I have faithfully serv'd and sung to you,
First as a groom, and anon as a knight so true –
Then grant me today my guerdon bright to know,
Forsooth, let me be the first to smite the foe.')
    Der Taillefer ritt vor allem Normannenheer
Auf einem hohen Pferde mit Schwert und mit Speer;
Er sang so herrlich, das klang über Hastingsfeld;
Von Roland sang er und manchem frommen Held.
(Foremost of all did Taillefer ride afield,
Upon a lofty charger, with sword and shield.
And cheerily swept his song o'er Hastings plain;
Of Rowland and knighthood brave he sang amain.)
    Und als das Rolandslied wie ein Sturm erscholl,
Da wallete manch Panier, manch Herze schwoll;
Da brannten Ritter und Mannen von hohem Mut;
Der Taillefer sang und schürte das feuer gut.

(The lay anent Rowland, it sounded like the storm,
And banners wav'd, and many a heart grew warm;
Then knight and vassal were nerv'd to deeds of might.
Ha! Taillefer sang and fann'd the fire aright!)
   Dann spreng' er hinein und führte den ersten Stoss,
Davon ein englischer Ritter zur Erde schoss,
Dann schwang er das Schwert und führte den ersten Schlag,
Davon ein englischer Ritter am Boden lag.
(Then onward he prick'd and gave the leading thrust:
As English champion needs must bite the dust.
Then he brandish'd his sword and gave the leading blow:
And again an English knight on earth lay low.)
   Normannen sahen's, die harrten nicht allzu lang,
Sie brachen herein mit Geschrei und mit Schilderklang.
Hei, sausende Pfeile, klirrender Schwerterschlag,
Bis Harald fiel und sein troziges Heer erlag!
(The Northmen saw it and charg'd across the field;
Onward they rush'd with shout and clashing shield.
How hurtled the arrow! How rang the falchionblade!
Till Harald and his bold vassals low were laid.)
   Herr Wilhelm steckte sein Banner aufs blutige Feld;
Inmitten der Toten spannt' er sein Gezelt;
Da sass er am Mahle, den gold'nen Pokal in der Hand,
Auf dem Haupte die Königskrone von Engelland.
(The Duke o'er the red field bid his banner wave,
And his tent he pitch'd among the dead and brave.
Then he sate at the feast with the golden cup in hand,
On his head the crown so kingly of England.)
   'Mein tapfrer Taillefer, komm, trink' mir Bescheid!
Du hast mir viel gesungen in Lieb' und in Leid;
Doch heut' im Hastingsfelde dein Sang und dein Klang,
Der tönet mir in den Ohren mein Leben lang.'
('Taillefer brave, come, drink me a pledge,' quoth he,
'In weal and woe thou hast serv'd and sung to me;
But to-day, on Hasting's field, thou sang'st a song
That shall ring in my ears, I ween, my whole life long').[2]

Strange, is it not, that I read this poem in my German textbook at school way north of the arctic circle in Norway? I could hardly have imagined that a few years later I was going to meet a distant relative of Taillefer.[3]

Who was Taillefer and how did the name Taillefer become Borlase, your family name?

The Bayeux Tapestry, the embroidery of wollen thread (red, yellow, two shades of green and three shades of blue) on a grey linen backing, sixty-five metres long and half a metre wide, tells the story of the Norman invasion of 1066. It was made in England in the decade after the invasion. The cultural and artistic context are linked to the tapestry fragments found at the Oseberg and Rolvsøy excavations in Norway.[4] We went together to look at this masterpiece in the town of Bayeux.

The Latin texts embroidered into the tapestry do not mention Taillefer by name and it does not make a distinct allusion to his presence among the six hundred and twenty-one male figures of the Tapestry. But it is beyond a reasonable doubt that Taillefer, described as a *jongleur* and a *chanteur* (minstrel), was a real person and part of King William's invasion force, not just a figure of romance. The night before the battle he sang passages from the *Chanson de Roland* and on the following day he 'juggles with his sword at the front line of the invading army' and rides out in front of the first attack, killing two Englishmen, before being himself cut down.[5]

This celebrated minstrel and soldier was William Taillefer, a descendant of the counts of Angoulême, the nobility created by King Charles (the Bald) in the ninth century. The first count was Wulgrin who was married to Rogerlinde, daughter of the Duke of Toulouse. He was followed by Alduin and then by William who took the name Taillefer and built the Chateau Taillefer in Angoulême. His grandson, the third Count, was also named William Taillefer and nicknamed *le chanteur*. It would seem that he, for reasons unknown, had been disinherited and bypassed in the succession and he had joined a contingent in support of William of Normandy.

King William II (1087–1100), son of William the Conqueror, granted to the Lord of the Castle of Talfer in Angoulême a Cornish estate in the parish of St Wenn.[6] Was this granted to the *chanteur's* son or another near relative? Is it reasonable to assume that the estate was given to the family in Angoulême for services rendered in the occupation of England in 1066, a reward for the spirit, courage and ultimate sacrifice of the *chanteur* at Hastings? Isabella Taillefer, Countess of Angoulême, married King John of England in 1200; the link between Angoulême and England was further enhanced.

We visited Angoulême together and walked down Rue Taillefer the year Nina attended Lycée Saint-Paul. We also went to St Wenn in Cornwall and searched for the estate. Very little remains of the early structure of the Taillefer residence but the original site is still easily identified. The first families bore the name Taillefer before they gave the name Borlase to their Cornish estate as the family name. The distinct family coat of arms, two hands pulling at a horseshoe against a backdrop of ermine, and the Latin motto (*Te digna sequere* – your merit, your worth, accompany you) have remained through the centuries.

Your name wandered far and wide from the beginnings in Cornwall at the end of the eleventh century, carrying the history and legends of the Counts of Angoulême, the heroism of the minstrel William and the allurement of Isabella, Queen of England with it.

Sir William Borlase who was a friend and contemporary of Ben Jonson painted a portrait of the playwright and sent it to him as a present with a verse beginning:

> To paint thy worth, if rightly I did know it,
> And were but painter half like thee, a poet;
> Ben, I would shew it.

Ben Jonson must have been pleased with the quality of the painting and he returned the compliment with 'The answer of the Poet to the Painter':

> ... when of friendship I would draw the face,
> A letter'd mind, and a large heart would place
> To all posterity, I would write Burlace.

Perhaps the family talent for fine art manifested itself during our stay in Japan in your gift for *sumie* (the writing and drawing with black ink), *byobu* (folding screen painting), and *ikebana* (the Japanese art of flower arrangement).

It was in the mining industry as engineers and managers that your more recent ancestors sought their fortune, first in Cornwall and then at the Greenside Lead Mine in Cumbria from 1825. Your great great grandfather, William Henry Borlase, and his sons William Henry Junior (your grandfather) and your great uncle Eddie Borlase were key players in the most succesful lead mine in the Lake District with continuous output for one hundred and forty years.[7]

Your grandfather was always on the move, perhaps searching for the perfect gold mine he never found and this drove him to other parts of the world, to Africa, South America and Canada. He was known to have 'a bit of a wanderlust'. Hence your father, Arthur, was born in North Bay, Sudbury, when your grandfather was manager of a large goldmine in Nova Scotia.

The ancestral mining genes seemed to reappear in your choice of geology, botany and geography for A-level at St. Julien's High School for Girls, Newport, achieving A (Distinction) from the University of Oxford Examination Body. You served as a senior school prefect at St. Julian's and studied the same subjects at the University of Exeter.

You had been offered a place to study at the University of Bristol but you chose Exeter where we would meet. Again fate, chance? Random chance becomes destiny?

NINETEEN

✦

You and I had been invited to a private dinner by the Department Head in Auswärtiges Amt for Britain and the Nordic Countries, Graf and Gräfin Norwin Leutrum v. Erlingen, in Wachtberg-Villiprott in Bonn, on 9 November 1989. During dinner the news filtered through that the Berlin Wall had fallen and that people from East Berlin were streaming towards the West. To the question 'Where were you when the Wall fell?' we would proudly answer that we were in a German home with German friends.

When the Party Secretary for East Berlin and member of the East German Polit-Bureau, Günter Schabowski, at a press conference in the evening of 9 November indicated free border crossings without stipulating the formal conditions and simply saying that the new travel regulations would enter into force immediately, the point of no return had been reached – by a slip of the tongue? Gorbachev has admitted that coincidences can dramatically accelerate an historical process.

Our four years in Germany were a kaleidoscope of events and people as God's steps echoed through the events and the Berlin Wall miraculously opened and the two halves of Germany united. I had been appointed to our Embassy in Bonn on 2 September 1988 and given responsibility for political affairs with rank as *Gesandter* (Minister), a rare opportunity for political reporting as history unfolded faster than the imagination.

On 9 April 1990, we were standing at the Berlin Wall. Fifty years earlier Germans forces had attacked Norway as a prelude to occupation. Was this finally the end of the punishment of Germany for the sins of the past? Sledgehammers had been used to break openings in the Wall and it was now possible to walk through. The DDR was still an independent state, but the guards turned away, controlling the passage now seemed absurd. The Wall was to become souvenir and museum and let Berlin rise again across the dividing line. We collected some pieces from the Wall.

The Germans in the West were to be teachers for the Germans in the East. This learning process included a reduction, restructuring and adaptation of the former Volksarmee in DDR. Officers and soldiers, screened and selected to be part of the new Bundeswehr of about 340,000, including 100,000 conscripts, faced a thorough re-education and readjustment. To retain German membership of NATO Moscow had demanded a considerable reduction in the total number of German forces.

I was given a rare chance to witness this re-orientation first hand as I was invited to participate in a series of lectures organized by the general headquarters of Divisions- und Wehrbereichskommando VII in Leipzig. In cooperation with my host, Major General Ekkehard Richter, I had chosen to speak on the elaborate democratic process guiding the Norwegian approach to membership of the EU. Democracy was the new watchword to be understood differently from the middle letter in DDR. In this process of military integration General Richter stood out as an ideal military diplomat for the unification of the two armies. Germany was no longer a front line state but surrounded by allied countries and partners.

You joined me on this most remarkable journey into the new, integrated Germany and we were received with courtesy and friendship by our hosts and given a memorable dinner at Gästehaus

Gräfesstrasse. We stayed at one of the former atmospheric DDR barracks in Sylter Strasse.

We understood better after briefings by the state government why the turning point (*die Wende*) in the reunification process had come in Saxony and Leipzig. The Monday demonstration march on 6 November 1989 from the St. Nikolai Church embraced half a million people who were repeating the line 'Deutschland einig Vaterland' from DDR's own national anthem.

Saxony was traditionally an energy region based on brown coal. The regime forced industrial development without environmental considerations or protection. The pressure on the population and the environment gradually became intolerable with increasing health problems and declining living and housing standards. Linked to this causality of industrial exploitation, history itself adds explanations to the front line role of Leipzig in 1989. Saxony and Leipzig had historically a strong separate identity, a pride in their own region, second to none opposite Prussia and Berlin. Leipzig was a cultural centre embracing a university and several colleges and displaying intellectual independence. The intellectuals had rebelled against Honecker's invitation to Ceauşescu in the autumn of 1988 and his opposition to Gorbachev's perestroika expressed on that occasion. The tearing down of the University Church in Leipzig in 1968 had made a deep impression in Leipzig and Saxony because a symbol of freedom had been removed, and this had in itself created distance to Ulbricht and Honecker.

In the years before *die Wende* the peace movement had met in the St. Nikolai Church and this core meeting expanded into the Monday demonstrations. The driving force behind *die Wende* in Leipzig was the release and the renewal of this independent intellectual tradition and a protest against the total exhaustion of the people through pollution and increasing poverty by a failing regime.

Willy Brandt's poignant words in Berlin on 10 November 1989 'Wir sind jetzt in der Situation wo zusammenwächst, was zusammengehört' (We are now in the situation where that which belongs together grows together) were later rewritten with equal poignancy in the language of the revue theatre in the new German eastern states 'Es wächst auseinander was zusammengehört' (What belongs together grows apart).

General Richter invited us to the cabaret theatre Academixer in Kupfergasse in Leipzig for the performance of 'Fahren(ge)lassen' (abandon{ed}), subtitled 'Eine kleine Auto-Biographie der Ossis', a revue in five acts about a journey by Trabi through Europe after reunification, a nostalgic and ironic comment on the new Germany. The colour on the western side of the Wall had seemed so bright but like a chameleon it changed when one got closer. Act one of the unification cabaret had just started as we watched. The Monday demonstrations in Leipzig would soon turn into demonstrations against unemployment and discrimination.

TWENTY

✦

One evening as we returned from a reception in Dar es Salaam we noticed one of the security guards sitting under one of the spotlights at the residence, quietly reading a book. You went over to him, curious to see what he was reading. To your surprise and delight he was studying *The Principles of Physical Geography* by Professor F.J. Monkhouse, a standard text book for students of Geography and as it happened a book that had been presented to you as a form prize at St. Julians High School in 1958.

The guard's name was Gift Wanangwa and he explained that he was trying to read for an external B.A. degree at the Open University of Tanzania while working as a security guard. We had employed a cook, a maid and two gardeners but we had also been looking for someone who could assist you in the organization of events and generally supervise in the running of the property. A few days later you and I offered him a position with the understanding that he would be given flexible time to prepare for the university courses and exams. He happily accepted this offer and became an excellent support. He was successful in his courses at the university. On 9 March 2000 Gift was conferred the B.A. degree by the Chancellor of the Open University of Tanzania, Dr. John Malacela.

The story of the houseboy at the Norwegian Residence made front-page news in Tanzania and even travelled to Kenya. *The East African* (Nairobi) referred to 'A story of hope and inspiration from Tanzania: A houseboy was among the 49 graduates conferred first degrees and certificates by the Open University of Tanzania.'

Your initiative and Gift's success were seen as an example in a letter to you from the Member of Parliament and Secretary General of the Union (UWT), Rhoda L. Kahatano:

On behalf of the Chairperson of UWT Mama Anna Abdallah, the leadership of the UWT and on my own behalf, I take this opportunity to sincerely thank you for having contributed to the success of Gift Wanangwa.

This is a rare instance and a very important and historical one. It will not only remain in Gift's memory but will be remembered by many Tanzanians who follow rare achievements of people like this one.

Our late father of the nation Mwalimu Julius Kambarage Nyerere always said, where there is a will there is a way, it can be done if you play your part. Here we are, Gift Wanangwa has done it, he is a graduate. You have played a very big role. We commend you for this very important contribution to one of our children who needed somebody to help him meet his ambition.

The Minister of Labour and Youth development, P.P. Kimiti, who had been the guest of honour at the Norwegian National Day Reception in 1999 and also attended the Degree Ceremony made the essential point to you and I: 'You could have walked past but you did not.'

When Gift and his girlfriend, who was a talented cook at the Residence, had a daughter they called her – Jill.

You had seen a flicker of light on an open book under a flame tree in Msasani Road at night.

☐

You had been a student of Africa for Geography A-level (1958–60) before the wind of change and independence for African nations and then again at university immediately after independence. Tanganyika had been a German colony, a British-administered League of Nations Mandate and a United Nations Trust Territory under British administration before independence in 1961.

You could take this knowledge of history, people (including the nomadic *Maasai*), politics, economics and physical features to our posting in Tanzania (so named after the union with Zanzibar in 1964).

After the usual procedures in our system, first my nomination by the Senior Officials Appointment Board in the Foreign Ministry, *agrément* (acceptance) by the Tanzanian government and appointment by the King in Cabinet 15 December 1995 you and I were due to start at the Embassy on 19 February 1996.

The day we were about to leave from the hotel in Oslo via London to Dar es Salaam I was asked to report to the Permanent Secretary in the Foreign Ministry and I received a prestigious message. The King and Queen of Norway with the Crown Prince and the Princess were to spend their Easter Holiday on safari in Tanzania concluded by an official visit and programme. The Permanent Secretary called the Palace and I was given an audience with the King the following day. The flights scheduled for Tanzania had to be altered. The King was clearly looking forward to a different Easter adventure. As we said good-bye he said with a smile: 'You now get a flying start.'

Soon after arrival I presented my accreditation letter to the President of Tanzania. This letter carries an elegant but archaic message from one head of state to another. As a teacher and phonetician of English you appreciated a language retained for a special protocol:

Dear and Good Friend,

Being desirous to maintain and strengthen the friendly relations which so happily subsist between the Kingdom of

Norway and the United Republic of Tanzana, I have appointed Mr. Nils-Johan Jørgensen as my Ambassador Extraordinary and Plenipotentiary to your Excellency.

The qualities which distinguish Mr. Jørgensen give me the assurance that he will discharge the duties of the Mission in such a manner as to merit Your Excellency's approbation and esteem.

I therefore request that Your Excellency will receive him with benevolence and give entire credence to all that he may communicate to your Excellency on My behalf and especially when he shall assure your Excellency of the high esteem and friendship with which I am,

Dear and Good Friend
Your Excellency's
Good Friend
Harald R

Security and privacy dictated that the Royal Visit, the destination as well as the programme, had to be kept secret by the Embassy until one week before the arrival. We succeeded in this.

□

In true tradition the Royal visit concluded with our reception for the Norwegian community in Tanzania.

It is fair to say that the electricity supply held a promise of uncertainty. On the morning of the reception we woke up early. The air-conditioning had turned off. We heard the guards outside arguing how to start the generator. Time passed. The electricity did not return and after close inspection it was concluded that the generator needed a new part to function again. This item had to be obtained from the manufacturer abroad. Not a very satisfactory state of affairs. The residence, the canapés and the drinks aligned with the ouside temperature of 34 degrees. After some heated negotiations with the electricity board we were reconnected in the nick of time and assured of uninterrupted supply for the day. The air-conditioning and the fridges resumed their operation and the reception was a success. The perfect hostess had taken cool control of the situation.

In the short time since our arrival you had made the residence fit for a King but you also turned it into a home. For the family it simply became Msasani Road.

I reminded you of Berthold Brecht's epigram 'Wahrnehmung' (perception): 'Die Mühen der Gebirge liegen hinter uns, vor uns liegen die Mühen der Ebenen' (The difficulties of the mountains are behind us, in front of us are the difficulties of the plains). We had climbed Kilimanjaro and ahead of us beckoned the long walk across Serengeti.

It would also mean social events galore at the house – a thousand guests per year. All this you handled with superb competence and elegance. I turn the pages of the Guest Book and marvel at the social activity you administered in six capitals on three continents.

☐

After the Royal Visit to Tanzania in 1996 I found it appropriate to recommend an official visit by the President of Tanzania and the First Lady to Norway. The President was invited by formal letter from the Norwegian Prime Minister. I handed the letter to the President and we discussed the framework for the programme in Norway. The visit was scheduled for 20–22 August.

You and I met the President and the First Lady and the Tanzanian delegation together with the Chief of Protocol at the military terminal at Fornebu Airport. After arrival a welcome Luncheon was hosted in honour of the President by the Minister for International Development, the outstanding Hilde Frafjord Johnson. This was followed by the President's lecture at the Norwegian Institute of International Affairs, political talks between the President and the Prime Minister, Press Conference and the official dinner at Akershus Castle hosted by the Prime Minister. A packed programme continued the following day. First a session in the Trade Council of Norway with representatives of Norwegian Industries, a meeting with the Committee of Foreign

Relations in Parliament before the King and Queen gave an audience for the President and the First Lady at the Royal Palace followed by the official Luncheon. In all this you and I had a front seat together. In addition you were hostess for the additional programme for the First Lady including Norwegian voluntary development organizations, children and family issues and art exhibitions.

The terrorist onslaught on the US Embassies in Nairobi and Dar es Salaam on 7 August 1998 (two weeks before the President's visit to Norway) provoked countermeasures from the Clinton administration and missiles were launched against targets in Afghanistan and Sudan – as it happened, on the first day of the President's visit in Oslo. High politics touched Oslo.

After the dinner at Akershus in Oslo, Secretary of State, Madeleine Albright, telephoned the President and explained the reaction based on intelligence reports that Osama bin Laden had been sighted at a definite location in Afghanistan and that chemical weapons of mass destruction were stored in a location in Sudan.

During the meeting at the Trade Council the next day as the President gave his speech, the PPS handed him a note. Apparently an excited President Mandela was on the phone arguing that Mkapa ought to return to Dar es Salaam for a regional discussion of the American misguided attack in Sudan against a civilian target. Mkapa was clear that he was not going to cut short his programme. It was a foretaste of the theme of terror that was going to be top of the agenda in the years to come.

□

The President and the First Lady invited us to a farewell Luncheon at their private apartment in State House on 20 June 2001. This was not common practice, indeed it was an exceptional honour and a recognition by the President, not only of the Embassy's handling of Norway's vast development programme but perhaps more significantly the ability to balance a critical analysis with a constructive political dialogue, not least in relation to Zanzibar. In this your social skills had been instrumental and you had developed a genuine rapport with the President and the First Lady.

As we were leaving, the President gave us a painting depicting a scene from Zanzibar.

In a meeting between the President and the diplomatic corps at State House I had, in the context of the war against corruption, quoted the line from T.S. Eliot's poem 'Burnt Norton': 'Time present and time past are both perhaps present in time future, and time future contained in time past.' The President, an English scholar, would immediately understand this as a pointed reference to the intransigence of the government party CCM. At the CG-meeting a few weeks later he referred to our exchange and replied by quoting from Shakespeare's *Julius Caesar*: 'There is a tide in the affairs of men, which, taken at the flood, leads on to fortune; omitted, all the voyage of their life is bound in shallows and in miseries.'

I had sent a copy of my farewell speech from my last reception to the President. When we met at State House he quoted from it and with a smile referred to my reference to act one two and three in the democratic development of Tanzania. Indeed the invitation might have been triggered by this inclusive speech that you had inspired:

On behalf of Jill and myself I welcome you to this, our farewell reception in Tanzania.

Tanzania has been good to us. I hope we have been able to give something back. But as a Norwegian poet says, when we get far enough out we are only at the beginning. Here, we are only at the beginning of a democratic reform process. I feel sure you can take this forward from a hesitant beginning and make Tanzania the example in Africa that Africa needs.

I know as Europeans we ask many questions but then I am reminded that the question mark is perhaps the most European of all punctuation marks. Let me just say that I respect that the question of Zanzibar is an internal matter and should be resolved internally, but, as good Europeans we must be permitted to ask questions. I met President Karume on 19

April this year with a delegation from the Norwegian Ministry of Foreign Affairs and this was a good meeting with good questions and good answers.

My Minister of International Development made some interesting remarks in her statement to the Norwegian Parliament this year. Let me first just briefly reflect on some of her points:

'Children, their welfare and their rights, come first in our development cooperation.

Norway is a small country, but an influential player in the area of development cooperation policy. And now we are richer than ever. Now it has become even more important for us to look beyond ourselves and our own particular interests.

Our resources, our knowledge and our values give us moral responsibility. We must share our wealth in order to promote growth and development in poorer countries. And if our own conscience does not spur us into action, someday our children will ask us, How much did you know? What did you do? Why didn't you do more?

The decline in development assistance provided by the wealthy countries during the 1990s coincided with the most ambitious reform movement ever launched by the developing countries. A good example of this is Tanzania. But the countries were in fact rewarded with less assistance than before. Norway therefore has a clear responsibility to increase its development assistance. Norway was the first to implement 100 per cent unilateral debt relief to the poorest countries. We aim to increase Norwegian development assistance to one per cent of the gross national product. We are nearly there.

The process of defining the main partner countries has begun based on the following factors: The countries must demonstrate a clear political will to solve major national problems themselves and promote good governance.'

We are again reminded that development assistance is a political issue. It requires brave policy choices at the national level in your country and in mine. I sent a copy of the

71

Minister's speech to President Mkapa and I am delighted to tell you that the President sent me a letter with the following assessment of the Minister's themes and I quote: 'It is an outstanding and sensitive statement of development cooperation policy, that has internalized the lessons and experiences of the first four development assistance decades, and charted what to me seems the correct approach for the future. I hope that the enlightenment argued here will catch on in the other OECD countries.' I could hardly receive a better and a more thoughtful message from your Head of State.

But now allow me to be an impressionist painter for a minute or two. Jill and I have visited the four corners of Tanzania, and more in our time here – Kigoma, Sumbawanga, Kasanga, Lindi, Arusha, Shinjanga not to mention Selous, Serengeti, Ngorongoro and even the Maasai village of Nainokanoka. Being a nomad myself like so many of you here this evening, and having lived in eight different countries, I am perhaps a Norwegian Maasai although my national costume is different.

My wife who has studied Geography, Geology and Botany, has never stopped telling me how particularly generous and creative God was when he designed Tanzania. Tanzania possesses the most varied geology and ecology of any country in Africa and virtually every crop known to agriculturalists will grow in Tanzania.

So what did we see? We have seen an old land where man first stood up and a young nation struggling to stand tall among nations. Some of you will have seen the shifting sands in Serengeti not far from Oldupai where man first made his footprints and wandered north. When we visited the Shifting Sands our younger daughter, Nina, was inspired to write a poem. If I may I would like to share it with you:

> A giant broom
> Sweeping sandy secrets
> Into a parched sea.

A one way tide
Chasing the wind
Over the edge
Of a flat Earth
Into the arms
Of a falling sun.
Arrested by space
In Oldupai
We touched
A floating key
Of Mahler's Fifth Symphony
And sailed
on the melody
Of our dreams,
As old as humanity.

This poem compares the impact of shifting sands to Mahler's 5th Symphony. Those of you who like to listen to music will recall that his symphony moves from darkness to light and the light is an exhilaration of life on earth.

And so we understand the poem better. It is a movement, shifting sand, from darkness to light. That is also what our combined effort in Tanzania is all about, to shift the sand year by year, to create light and fairness for the children of this country. That is the melody of their dreams, the light of education, the light of knowledge for every child. Our Norwegian national day is a children's day. Every Norwegian child is given the chance of education. That is the challenge for Tanzania to give her children the same chance. That is their human right. My elder daughter, Lisa, tells me that Africa asks for so little except that you shake its hand. But we cannot wish development more than does the country itself. We cannot wish dialogue between the parties in the union more than the parties do themselves. Above all, put Tanzania and its future first in all your efforts. Learn to lift and carry together as a nation.

There is a growing debate and opinion out there that aspects of traditional culture in Africa may act as obstacles to development and one of the points made is that the focus is too much on the past and the present and too little on the future. I hope this point can be disproved and that you may take Tanzania towards a better future. The African renaissance is essentially a birth and a discovery of modern democratic political systems more than a rebirth and rediscovery of African cultures and your creative past. The President's reform process points in the right direction. If time future is contained in time past the past must now release the future.

The fight for democracy is the greatest drama of our time. Democracy does not pop up easily and ready-made. It would be foolish to think so. Perfect democracies are relatively rare in the world today. The struggle for a modern democracy has been going on in Tanzania only since the introduction of the pluralist society in 1992 and the first multi-party elections in 1995 and last year. What was true at first light must not be a lie at noon. The play is on the stage, act one, 1995, and act two, 2000, are behind us, act three, 2005, is yet to be written and played. The question whether act one was better than act two is academic, the challenge before us is in 2005.

Democracy is an evolving process; the key is to have a system in place before the next election to which all parties can agree. A free and fair election is the foundation for good governance, the fight against corruption and development. The difficult part is to take your internal dialogue from confrontation towards consensus. In May this year the UN marked the Freedom of the Press Day for the tenth time. A free press and media have an essential part to play in enhancing democracy. I wish you success both in staging and acting act three in 2005. The important point is that the next election holds the key to your democratic future. We will watch the play and ask questions. Your people will watch the play and ask questions. We cannot give you the answer. Only you have the answer.

As the ambassador is sent to lie abroad, his wife and children will tell the truth. I have also let you know what they think. And I finally ask you the difficult question: Can you be the example? Can you give the reform process the dedication it needs? If so, that would give you real power as a nation at home and abroad.

And so from the four of us I thank you again for all you have given us and I wish you a tide in the affairs of Tanzania, a time future of step-by-step progress.

In his reply the Minister for Good Governance, Wilson Masilingi, included you:

I would like to thank Your Excellency, for your critical contribution towards strengthening the relations between Tanzania and Norway. You have been so wonderful and we are going to miss you a lot. Your advice was always well balanced and constructive. We thank you once more for being honest in your words and deeds. We are also thankful to your wife, Jill, for her contribution and for giving you support during your stay in Tanzania.

The representative of the World Bank, Jim Adams, sent this e-mail to us:

Having read the speech a number of times I wanted to say how touched I was with it. The statement combined humility, optimism, vision and wisdom – not an easy combination and particularly rare in diplomatic circles. To look beyond the problems of today and ask the really difficult questions is never easy. To do it with style and grace is an accomplishment indeed. In addition, to inject the wisdom of your wife and daughters made it all the more powerful. I just hope Tanzania is listening – I am always concerned most of the donors are too short sighted and too focused on their concerns, rather than Tanzania's. That you were able to express so well your love of

Tanzania with your concerns makes it a piece that everyone in government should read and reflect upon. I know I will be recommending it as required reading.

The First Secretary for infrastructure (roads, water and energy), Arne Olsen, representing the Embassy at our last farewell reception, gave us a speech we would remember with melancholy joy:

It is a fact that you will be leaving the Embassy and Tanzania by the end of this month. I am afraid there is nothing we can do about that. What we can do is to assure you that we will miss you very much. Especially your good spirits. (I am not talking about the drinks at your house.) Your sense of humour, your unpolished jokes from Northern Norway, your smile and your laughter have all been trademarks of the Norwegian Embassy in Dar during your reign here. We will miss that.

Professionally, I think you can safely be characterized as a political animal. You seem to like it most when you can feed on, and feed into, political processes of some complexity. I guess that is a talent that has been nurtured over your long career in the Foreign Service. You have a gift to grasp the essential feelings of the parties involved. Combine that with your networking capabilities and you have the reason why you have been a recognized and appreciated partner in the political picture in Tanzania. One particular example stands out, and that is Zanzibar. It is an issue where your judgement has been proven correct, and where you can safely be said to have made a difference.

As we all know, development cooperation in Tanzania and political development go hand in hand. You have succeeded in integrating policy issues into your development efforts in a way that is highly respected both by the government of Tanzania, by the other donors, as well as by the other Norwegian embassies and Norad and the ministry back home. In fact, when I was in Oslo last week I was told several times: 'The Embassay in Dar es Salaam is one of the best-run embassies we have.' We should all be honoured and proud by such a statement, but special honour and pride should be taken by the top man, that is you.

An Ambassador ought not to take farewell sentiments too seriously but in the words of Jonathan Swift: "Tis an old maxim in schools that flattery's the food of fools; yet now and then your men of wit, will condescend to take a bit.'[1] The farewell sentiments from Wilson, Jim and Arne together with the private Luncheon with President and Madame Mkapa gave us an evaluation that we would happily like to recognize and believe.

You maintained the optimism, vision and wisdom in a post full of challenges and intense activity. We had the honour of receiving the King and Queen of Norway in 1996 and again to accompany the President of Tanzania and the First Lady to Norway in 1998. The successful outcome on both occasions was not least due to your practical and diplomatic skills. But it was in the time in between, in the role as the Ambassador's wife at a large Embassy, in the hard slog to keep a high standard at the residence in a hardship post in a developing country, that your character and spirit stood the test. The many guests who came to the home would bear witness to that. The diplomatic service 'requires partners to make significant sacrifices financially, in career terms and in their ability to have a normal family existence ... They are willing to put up with such harsh conditions because they are committed to making a difference, to improving the world around us.'[2]

You made the difference.

TWENTY-ONE

✦

The girl who looked at us for the first time one early spring morning in Oslo and travelled with us to distant shores told us she was getting married. Had time passed so quickly? To honour that we had been married on the nineteenth day of the month, Lisa chose Sunday 19 December 1999. Family and friends from many parts of the world gathered at the Sea Cliff Hotel in Dar es Salaam, prominent among them my own mother, Johanna, born in 1912.

On the day, they arrived at the residence for drinks in the garden before they gathered under the big flame tree for the civil ceremony. I was entitled to be the solemnizer. Lisa had wished that. It was an emotional moment.

You wore a wide, beautiful hat – perfect under the sun. I called it the spinnaker. I know you understood. We would now be running before the wind without Lisa, the permanent crew member. Not long ago Lisa had held our hand as she walked towards new dicoveries and I always knew that 'all my life I'll feel a ring invisibly circle this bone with shining'.[1] Just as you would.

I had to remind the bride and groom, in accordance with the official text that 'vowing to love each other for the rest of your life is the most difficult promise you can make to another person'. How strange that the ritual wisdom has to insist that this is so difficult. It had been the easiest promise for me to keep in the whole world – 'loving her was easier than anything I'll ever do again'.[2]

After the formal civil ceremony, we continued to St Peter's Chapel, The Missions to Seamen, in Kurasini, for the Blessing Service conducted by the Reverend Father Joachim Lieberich, the Port Chaplain for the Apostleship of the Sea. The ceremony included a reading from Song of Songs. Norway had financed the Dogo Dogo Centre Street Children Trust, the project to support the 3,000 street children in Dar es Salaam, providing education and employment. Lisa asked the Dogo Dogo Centre Choir to sing at the church ceremony including the evergreen *Malaika* and the national anthem (*Mungu ibariki Tanzania* – God bless Tanzania).

The same evening we held the reception and dinner at the residence. You had organized as a surprise a performance of traditional music and dancing as guests arrived. You created a most perfect setting for Lisa on this her special day with a careful attention to detail – as always. As we sat down to dinner you said a few words of welcome. It was time for my speech from you and I. It was a wishing-well, from both of us and I began with a line from *The Merchant of Venice* reflecting our first spring in 1961:

The moon shines bright. In such a night as this, when the sweet wind did gently kiss the trees ...

Lisa kept us guessing when she was actually going to be born – 10p.m., midnight, 1a.m. oh no, 4.30 in the morning if you please. The time of the toughest watch for any soldier or seaman but then there she was with big eyes silently saying 'Hi daddy what are you doing here?' The point is probably this: To a parent the child is all ages at once. You see her as grown up, I see her also as a new born child, a schoolgirl and a teenager.

A popular song at the time of her birth was 'I beg your pardon I didn't promise you a rose garden'. No, we could not offer Lisa a stable garden but a nomadic life and many different gardens in Oslo, Bruxelles, Copenhagen, Harare,

Tokyo, Bonn, St Andrews, Canterbury, Oxford, London and now in Dar es Salaam. It has been said that between two countries you have none at all. So what do you get beween eight?

Lisa sent me a card once with the text 'Hard work got you where you are, where are you?' and on the other side you had written 'We got there together.' Not a bad summing up. Lisa was destined to be a camp follower. But that makes us the original people. In the beginning was the migrant. The word pilgrim has two meanings in Latin – peregrinus – stranger and perager – one who lives abroad. As Schiller says 'A restless wandering was our life, homeless like the wind.' You became what the Japanese would call *kikokushijo* or what the German calls *Grenzgänger* and *Grenzüberschreiter*. We cross borders and time zones. After the first day in Kindergarten in Copenhagen having just come from Bruxelles you waved your little hand and said 'sådan, voila'.

Lisa had to break up from temporary homes that often seemed to have what you wished to remain. Once you owned a horse called Magic that took you over high fences. But he could not travel with you over time zones. You wrote a story about that in the school magazine in Tokyo and mothers read it to their children and it made them cry.

I referred to Lisa's open eyes at birth and you will notice her big eyes today. It therefore seems natural having referred to her nomadic life to recall Athene in *The Odyssey*, the lady with the gleaming and beautiful eyes. I recall a scene in Bruxelles when Lisa was about two and a colleague took a good look at her eyes and said 'Those eyes will trouble some boy one day.' And they did and here we are. Richard has been troubled as sometimes from her eyes (he) did receive fair speechless messages. Lisa's eyes can smile like sunrise and the midnight sun and they can flash like lightning in a storm.

We gather here tonight and we may seem to be part of a plan or are we just part of chance – playthings of the gods? I would like to tell you a story. Early in the last century my great-great grandfather Jørgen married Lava. They had two

80

daughters. He was a fisherman and was out there in the Lofoten Islands in December trying to make a living. He had just built a house for his family at a place called Skarstein across the sea from the old Viking Island of Bjarkøy. When he arrived home the house was empty. His wife and the children had crossed the sound between the two islands to visit her brothers. Sailing back a crosswind capsized the boat. They were never found. Many years later my great grandfather married again and they had four children. One of them was my grandfather. So you see Lisa is here because of a crosswind in 1852. Fate, chance, destiny. The mystery is out there and it remains. All of you here can tell similar stories.

I would now like to tell you another story from another time zone. A long time ago, Buddha, called all the animals of the world to him. Only twelve came, the rat, the ox, the tiger, the rabbit, the dragon, the snake, the horse, the sheep, the monkey, the cock, the dog and the boar. Each animal that had come to that reception received from Buddah as a mark of honour a year in their name and each animal contributed its characteristics to that particular year. According to Japanese belief therefore from these twelve zodiac symbols a person's fortune may be told, the character, strength, weaknesses, talents – the course of that person's life.

Now, Lisa, according to this Japanese fortune calendar, is born in the year of the boar and she is therefore both chivalrous and gallant. Also, people in the year of the boar do what they must with all the strength they have for their strength is an inner strength that no one can overcome. There is no retreat when a boar person sets out to do something with tremendous fortitude and great honesty. They make friends for life and they have a great thirst for knowledge. As an anthropologist and a nomad, this thirst for knowledge is not tied to one culture because of culture. Lisa's field trips as a student to Svalbard, Japan, Tahiti, Italy and Southern Africa are cases in point. It also showed her inner strength and fortitude, having to rely on herself.

81

This afternoon you made a commitment and a promise, a pledge to love and to be faithful and to remain two independent and equal individuals. Love and unity also means freedom, autonomy and respect.

And as we wish you luck I recall what the priest said to my parents when they got married in a different time zone in the old Viking Trondenes Church in Northern Norway – Be of one mind and be at peace with one another (*Ha ett sinn, og hold fred med hverandre*). Perhaps he simply meant don't waste your precious time together, look for the bigger picture. Like true Renaissance people have your eyes fixed on the stars. Find the magic out there. Create your little society, a society where none intrudes. And you may then with the poet say to one another that all you need as you set sail is A Book of Verses underneath the Bough, 'A Jug of Wine, a Loaf of Bread – and Thou'.[3]

A toast to Lisa and Richard from Jill and I.

My mother, Johanna Marie, kept a diary from Lisa's wedding and her visit to Tanzania. You could not have known her final words in the diary, written after you flew together to Heathrow at the end of January 2000: 'Unforgettable Jill. Your thoughtful consideration. The world was yours and a part of it was also mine. Thank you.'

The way you were. A few words that say it all. My mother who passed away in 2008 never recovered from your death and spoke of you and her visit to Tanzania until the end.

My mother's funeral was in the winter in Northern Norway but the sun had reappeared. The sea was dead calm. The snow covered the mountains, the fields and the town. The sun made the snow sparkle into a thousand stars, like a cosmic dance brought to earth. The day of the funeral I woke to a beautiful, sunny day, everything clad in white.

The parson, Lars Martin Skipevag, spoke with the greatest love and respect about Johanna and her life based on her own writing. He reflected on the sentiment that she always gave of her time, referring to your speech to my mother at her 90th birthday party.

To keep you with me, in the same church where we held the memorial service for you, I repeated what my mother had said about you in her diary.

At the end, six of us carried Johanna to the waiting car for a last drive across the white surface as if she was now turning into white flowers. Johanna Marie would have appreciated the speeches and the company and Lars Martin's eulogy. Yes, she would have liked that.

But she would still not have understood why you were not there with me.

TWENTY-TWO

✦

We celebrated our thirtieth wedding anniversary in the Seychelles,'a thousand miles from anywhere'. This Eden of 115 islands in the Indian Ocean was sighted by the Arabs and then by the Portuguese early in the sixteenth century but the first recorded landing was by the English East India Company in 1609. In 1742 the French Governor of Mauritius sent Captain Lazare Picault to explore the islands. France took possession in 1756, the archipelago was ceded to Britain in 1814 and gained independence in 1976. Only twenty-one of the country's islands are inhabited today. We obtained the official first day cover of the eight stamps of 29 June 1976. We went to the National Archives at Mahé and saw the first plans of settlement.

I was also appointed Norway's Ambassador to Seychelles from Dar es Salaam (a rare bonus) and presented my accreditation letter to President France Albert René in State House 21 November 1996. After the official programme, including a Luncheon given by the Government in State House, we flew to Pralin to explore the Vallee de Mai and to visit Kari and Roald Nilsen, the only Norwegians on the islands, a former Sandinavian Airlines Captain who at that time was flying for Air Seychelles and had established Praslin Ocean Farm and developed a unique Seychellois Pearl.

84

We landed on the small grass strip on Bird Island, north-west of Mahé, to view the concentration of various tern species also found on two other islands of seabirds, Aride and Cousin. It was a spectacle like the bird scene in the novel *Silk*[1] and the reference to the custom when a Japanese man would honour the love and faithfulness of his sweetheart by giving her an exquisite bird instead of jewels. The *hototogisu* bird of Kyoto appears frequently as a symbol of love in *Kōkinshū*.

I continued my official contact with Seychelles in the following years until in June 2001 it was time to ask for a farewell audience with the President. We invited over one hundred guests to the farewell reception at Fisherman's Cove with the Foreign Minister as guest of honour. The Permanent Secretary of the Ministry of Foreign Affairs gave us a book on the world heritage site, Aldabra, the world's largest raised coral atoll and one of the wonders of the world (according to David Attenborough), and you immediately put it out for signatures by the guests. On the same occasion I decorated the Norwegian Honorary Consul with the Royal Order of Merit.

As we returned to our hotel room after the reception we found that a Coco de Mer with greetings from the Foreign Minister had been delivered. This double coconut from Vallee de Mai in Pralin, from the Tree of Knowledge in the Garden of Eden according to the legend, was unknown in Europe before the Portuguese explorations. It was first mentioned by Antonio Pigafetta in his account of Magellan's first voyage round the world and it was believed to grow in and even under the sea before it was discovered in Pralin in 1768. The coconut was believed to be an aphrodisiac, to contain medical properties and prevent illness. Emperor Rudolf II offered four thousand gold florins for one coco de mer and they were collected and treasured in royal circles throughout Europe. The coconut looks like the shapely buttocks and thighs of a woman. As we walked through immigration and customs on our return in Nairobi my hand baggage was x-rayed. I was politely asked what this was and I honestly insisted that it was only *une noix fabuleuse*.[2] Diplomatic language.

☐

You gave this irreverent epistolary impression of our journeys to the tropical garden paradise:

We had been in the East African/West Indian Ocean region almost nine months prior to embarking on the trip to Seychelles. A cursory glance at the map reinforced my casual thoughts; yes, Seychelles, more or less due west of Dar, distance, well, similar to a flight southern – northern Norway, say, two hours at the most. However, there were no direct flights to Seychelles, from Dar es Salaam. So much for my optimism of a short journey. It was to be via Nairobi and on the afternoon of the 12 November 1996 we left with Kenya Airways.

At the airport we were met by the Norwegian policeman seconded to the Embassy in Nairobi and later to Dar es Salaam. The following hour and a half was spent confirming the next stage of the journey Nairobi – Victoria with Air Seychelles scheduled for 0900 hours the following day. Having come straight from the humidity of coastal Dar es Salaam it was good to be in the high veld Nairobi air.

The next day the airport bus from the hotel left as planned at 0730 and we knew that there would be ample time for the checking in formalities at the airport. In fact we were about the first to arrive and it took some time before anyone would point us in the direction of the Air Seychelles check-in. After a while some Spanish passengers found their way towards us followed by others. The conversation was animated, something was amiss; the aircraft (we learned, ex-Madrid) was not coming. Two Kenya Airways ground staff had quietly appeared behind the check-in desk, but people talked of an indefinite delay of this particular flight. After a while we managed to get down to more reasonable facts; the aircraft had been declared unserviceable in Madrid and there would be an 18-hour delay on the subsequent departure out of Nairobi.

Trying to re-locate the passengers back into hotels was a headache airline staff did not need and it was 12.30 before we were heading back to the hotel with the prospect of having to leave again at 0200 a.m.

What does stand out in the mind was the way in which the bus driver manipulated his vehicle back to the airport at high speed.

We finally approached Victoria at 0800 on 14 November in a dazed state but as the aircraft turned finals there was no mistaking where we were; as far as the eye could see there was crystal clear azur blue sea, almost indistinguishable from the sky; it couldn't be difficult to be a pilot in such conditions as these surely? We were to learn otherwise a few days later. Anyway, the journey from Dar es Salaam had taken the best part of 42 hours and we were delighted to be in Seychelles.

Our stay included a visit by Twin Otter to one of the other islands, Praslin. The day dawned fine and hot and we were clad accordingly. On the landing strip we were met by the only resident Norwegian in Seychelles and driven to his home nearby to meet his wife and to see the giant clam project they have undertaken on the island since leaving Norway 10 years ago. At the end of a most interesting, but increasingly wet day, we returned to the departure lounge at the little airstrip, only to be left waiting while more and more passengers packed themselves into the limited area. But no flights as the fog thickened. We did get back having actually enjoyed yet another enforced night-stop.

All too soon our time ran out in Seychelles and we had to think about the return to Dar es Salaam. This time though it was going to be easy. There would be transit in Nairobi for a couple of hours only before going direct to Dar. It was an early departure from Victoria and that might have added to the chaos when boarding. Whether the aircraft was overbooked or not, the seat allocation system fell apart, so much so that we spent the two and a half hour flight to Nairobi marvelling that we and our baggage were on board at all. Possibly the

Egyptian Ambassador wished otherwise as in spite of his first class ticket he was placed at the extreme rear of the aircraft. On boarding, his briefcase was snatched out of his hand and shoved into an overhead locker right at the front.

We parted company with the Egyptian Ambassador in Nairobi and wished him well on his onward flight with Egypt Air to Cairo. Our policeman was there to meet us again and we related the hiatus of driving at top speed through Nairobi in the dead of night ten days previously. We subsequently learnt that this was the most dangerous time to be moving around in the city as crime, hijackings, ambushes etc. were all too frequent. We had been on a bus loaded with luggage.

We had about three hours to wait before the connection to Dar so we went to see the former home of Karen Blixen. It had been nostalgic to see the film Out of Africa in Japan after leaving Zimbabwe in 1984.

On our return to the airport we made for the lounge. In the absence of any announcements we made some tentative enquiries. 'Yes, that's right, you should have been airborne by now but there doesn't seem to be an Air Tanzania aircraft around and we don't know where it is,' stated the Kenya Airways representative at the information desk in the lounge. 'But don't worry, an Air Tanzania ground staff member will be here in due course and he might have some news.'

About half an hour later, the representative appeared on the scene in rather a confused state. 'All communication links with Dar es Salaam are out of action so we can't contact them but we have heard that there is an aircraft in Mwanza – the problem is that there has been a bad strike there so we don't know what's going on.' I asked him to repeat what he'd just said because although I couldn't quite understand what an aircraft in Mwanza had to do with us sitting in Nairobi, it was the cause of the problem with this aircraft that I couldn't figure out.

Nils-Johan had half continued to read The Herald Tribune but he'd got the gist of our exchange and became interested in the Mwanza aircraft too; 'What kind of strike did you say?' 'A bad strike, sir.' 'A what strike?' 'You know sir, when a bird flies into the engine.' Well we'd got that one sorted out. The aircraft in Mwanza had not been grounded by a bad strike. O.K. so we know that Air Tanzania has a fleet of two Boeing 737 aircraft, so where was the other one? 'In the hangar sir.' 'Which hangar?' 'Dar es Salaam, sir, but we can't contact them because Dar isn't answering.'

A good two hours later we were on our way; the aircraft had finally arrived in Nairobi. Then the crew took us round by Zanzibar. No one had said that this route had a stop-over in Zanzibar. We reached the clove island just as the sun was setting and by the time we were huddled into the transit room, darkness had fallen. My husband spied a mosquito on his leg and for the next hour he was trying to protect me and himself against the most scheming and silent of warriors. And then, the announcement came, unfortunately, we might be here indefinitely because all the lights had gone out in Dar es Salaam and the airport generator had packed up – hence there were no runway lights in operation. The mosquitos had a field night. However, half an hour later we seemed to be saved; lights back on and so with the Tanzanian capital once again flood-lit we could re-join the flight. Once we were strapped in, nothing happened; the cabin staff looked distraught and looked to their weary passengers for encouragement. The lights across the sea had failed again and once more we disembarked, to the delight of the waiting mosquitos.

It took another hour before we were finally airborne and 20 minutes later descended into Dar es Salaam. Not long afterwards the whole place was pitched into darkness again.

A year later, we set out for Seychelles once more. One of our daughters had starting working there in October and it had been decided that if my husband could arrange his official duties in the islands sometime in December, we would all have an opportunity of spending a Christmas holiday in this geographical paradise.

We set out from Dar es Salaam on 15 December and witnessed the magnificent African dawn over Tanzania from an altitude of 25,000 ft. on the Sunday Kenya Airways flight to Nairobi

British Airways had re-routed the previous direct London – Seychelles flight to make a transit stop, with traffic rights, in Nairobi and so this time we descended onto this beautiful island aboard a Boeing 747. The aircraft may have been different, but the jewel-like granite land forms rising out of the azur blue waters which contain abundant aquatic life, were just as inspiring as ever. Yes indeed, Paradise Unlimited to quote the brochures. The weary passengers who had travelled all night from a Europe in the grip of winter uttered a thankful sigh as their feet touched the tarmac and their heads felt the power of the tropical sun.

Apart from the usual ground staff attending to the aircraft on its stand, there were two other figures standing some distance from the base of the steps – our daughter and the Norwegian Honorary Consul. There have been many greetings and farewells with our family over the decades in our service, but it occurred to me that my daughter had never looked so well and in total harmony with herself and her environment.

For all the potential health hazards which living and working in the tropics can entail, there is certainly one bonus – the sun seems to come on the inside. Our Tanzanian maid at the residence in Dar never failed to tell me that 'you are too white mama' each time I returned from summer holidays in Norway and the U.K. (This can be modified slightly, bearing in mind that Kiswahili speakers frequently use 'too' where we would use 'very'.)

We moved into a bungalow on the eastern coast which we had agreed 'to mind' while the owners spent Juletide in their native Australia. Our house minding included among other things, looking after their three dogs which turned out to be quite a tall order. It was during the three weeks we looked after this house that we were afforded a glimpse into life in this paradise which boasts one of the highest per capita incomes in Africa. It is a well known fact that the Seychelles economy thrives on tourism; this accounts for nearly 70% of the total foreign exchange of the country although over the past decade the government has embarked on policies to develop the fisheries and off-shore sectors which aim at diversification of the economy to prevent over reliance on tourism.

Seychelles is very selective in the kind of tourists it wishes to attract and the costly holidays offered by European and South African tour operators are only within the grasp of the few; the high-yield tourist or big spenders are the target market, the back-packers are not. We could hardly be classified as the obvious luxury hotel resident when we were seen loaded with a week's shopping. While tourists basked on the palm-fringed beaches we were trying to make sense of the fruit and vegetable prices in Victoria's main city market. Almost all this perishable produce was imported from South Africa and Kenya. Similarly, the majority of the products in the downtown supermarket hailed from the U.K.

Having experienced Seychelles as ordinary consumers and come to the conclusion that the paradise is expensive, I should add that we have lived in one of the hotels along the Beau Vallon beach when my husband presented his credentials to the President.

While we were in the Seychelles we took a direct flight to Port Louis in Mauritius to present The Order of Merit to the Norwegian Honorary Consul.

Back again in Seychelles we started to prepare for Christmas in the bungalow we were looking after. The heat generated while cooking the turkey will be remembered for many Christmases to come.

In April 1984, during our posting in Zimbabwe, we had paid a visit to the Seychelles. On the return journey, with a Kenya Airways Boing 707, we experienced a Dutch Roll over the Indian Ocean, halfway between Victoria and Nairobi. Such incidents occur when the autopilot suddenly cuts out and the aircraft is exposed to a sudden lateral oscillation involving yaw, roll and sideslip. It was a dramatic scene with screaming passengers and objects flying around in the cabin but the pilots gained control and took the aircraft down to a lower altitude and landed without further incidents.

You kept the calmness of the former air-hostess but I could detect that you did not like this one bit.

Never a dull moment in Paradise.

TWENTY-THREE

✦

On his reurn to Ithaca, disguised as a wreched beggar, Odysseus is recognized by his faithful dog Argos who lifts his head and ears on hearing his master's voice. But Argos had been neglected during Odysseus' long absence and was now confined on a heap of dung. As he saw Odysseus close by and knew him, he wagged his tail and dropped his ears but he was unable to move. Odysseus glanced aside and wiped away a tear. Then the fate of dark death fell on Argos suddenly when he had once again set eyes upon Odysseus.

As a young lawyer, George Graham Vest, senator for Missouri (1879–1903), represented a client who had sued his neighbour for killing his dog. Vest won the case after this tribute to fidelity:

Gentlemen of the jury.
The best friend a man has in the world may turn against him and become his enemy. His son or daughter that he has reared with loving care may prove ungrateful. Those who are nearest and dearest to us, those whom we trust with our happiness and our good name may become traitors to their faith. The money that a man has, he may lose. It flies away from him,

93

perhaps when he needs it most. A man's reputation may be sacrificed in a moment of ill-considered action.

The people who are prone to fall on their knees to do us honour when sucess is with us may be the first to throw the stone of malice when failure settles its cloud upon our heads.

The one absolutely unselfish friend that man can have in this selfish world, the one that never deserts him, the one that never proves ungrateful or treacherous is his dog.

A man's dog stands by him in prosperity and in poverty, in health and in sickness. He will sleep on the cold ground, where the wintry winds blow and the snow drives fiercely, if only he may be near his master's side. He will kiss the hand that has no food to offer; he will lick the wounds and sores that come in an encounter with the roughness of the world. He guards the sleep of his pauper master as if he were a prince.

When all other friends desert, he remains. When riches take wings, and reputation falls to pieces, he is as constant in his love as the sun in its journey through the heavens.

If fortune drives the master forth an outcast in the world, friendless and homeless, the faithful dog asks no higher privilege than that of accompanying him, to guard him against danger, to fight against his enemies. And when the last scene of all comes, and death takes his master in its embrace and his body is laid away in the cold ground, no matter if all other friends pursue their way, there by the graveside will the noble dog be found, his head between his paws, his eyes sad, but open in alert watchfulness, faithful and true even in death.

We have owned two dogs. The first was a boxer called Toby. He travelled with us from Harare to Tokyo and then to Bonn. The second, Monty, came from Dar es Salaam to Sarre. Our Italian colleague in Dar es Salaam owned a boxer, imported from Italy, who got friendly with a local dog referred to as a Labrador and the result was a special breed of puppies. We obtained one of them and in conversation with the local veterinary, who also adopted one, it was suggested that the Labrador mother probably had genetic links to the now endangered Serengeti wild dog, called the painted dog (*lycaon pictus*) because each dog has unique markings. The Serengeti wild dog lives in packs of ten or more. The striking aspect is the social cooperation, cohesion, interaction and communication in the group. Before these dogs set out for a hunt they have a ceremonial meeting distributing tasks and responsibilities within the pack with special attention to the feeding and protection of the pups.

Toby and Monty were real companions in diplomacy, communicators and negotiators.

Monty had to endure quarantine for half a year. The choice is always either to leave the dog behind or let him come on the journey as a trailing dog. Nina reflected on this dilemma in a short story, *Toby's travels,* for the school magazine in Tokyo, a journey between Harare and Tokyo, via Heathrow and Anchorage, from his perspective:

My eyes flicked from one box to another, as they travelled in and out of the glass doors belonging to the dining room. I looked longingly at a piece of tape dragging along the ground, but seeing Lisa cast a warning glance in my direction, eliminated my plans of attack.

I lay in bed, puzzled, that night. Something was happening. Why else would the house be emptying so rapidly? If only I knew.

The next day, I bounded into the car, gleefully, happy at the thought of a ride. I was surprised when I found my favourite clothes and toys follow me. At the end of an hour I was bored, and enjoyed the chance to stretch out properly before noticing my surroundings. A lot of discussion and signing of forms went on among the grown-ups. Before I knew it, I was pushed through a gate, and, to my horror, saw millions of others in my situation. The moments that followed then seemed like a dream to me, and although I try to remember, I go blank. I do know that there was a lot of hugging and kissing and tears soaking my skin, and then I was alone.

I was unhappy during the weeks that followed, although I

had plenty of exercise and healthy food, and I met many new friends – and enemies. But the love of a family was missing, and as the days turned into weeks and months, I wondered if I would ever see them again.

One morning, I was woken up especially early, and was given my regular food and daily exercise. I then allowed myself to be hoisted onto a truck, and, glad at the thought of a new adventure, did not reflect when once again my belongings joined me. I slept for most of the journey, so I could not estimate the time it took, but I was woken by an enormous roar, and found the sky alive with huge, winged machines.

I shivered in fear and was led into a large building. Crowds of people swarmed around me, but I was pushed gently into a small room. Some mumbling went on at the desk, and soon I found myself face to face with a large, rounded wooden box. When asked to enter, I thought it had gone too far. I swirled round and retreated to the far corner of the room, eying my rivals suspiciously. But soon a horde of humans joined them, and I was inched slowly towards the box. The door slammed. I felt a nauseating feeling of claustrophobia, and slumped down. It was all I could do to keep down my breakfast when, during the next hour, I was carried and jolted around until I came to rest at the back of one of these mammoth birds.

Suddenly the bird began to shake, and an engine roared. I was filled with panic and jumped up. The top of the wooden box held me down, and the bang I received on my head acted as a sedative. I flung backwards and felt a rising feeling until the bird levelled out and I could relax. By that time it was late at night, and I realized that I had had nothing to eat since breakfast.

Later on someone came in while I was sleeping and pushed a bowl of water and some meat through the door. I attacked the food hungrily.

When I next woke up, I found that my half full water bowl had disappeared and that we were descending rapidly. I lurched forward, as the bird hit the ground with a shake.

After a long wait, and never a pat or a few kind words, I relived my previous adventures, but this time, as it was daytime, I was bored stiff. I received a small lunch and water, and then slept until it was time to land again. When I awoke, it was cold, and my ears felt like balloons, about to burst. On landing, I was in agony, and my ears popped, sending shudders through my body. This time I was not taken off onto land, and before I knew it we were ascending again into the air. I shivered, and was grateful when a person brought me some warm milk. Again, I slept, and dreamt that I was lying under the shade of my favourite tree at home, and the sun was beating down all around me. The dream turned into a nightmare, people were whipping and chasing me until I fell off the land and floated higher and higher into the sky. I woke with a start. I was boiling, and thirsty, and once again found that we were descending. After landing, I was hauled off the monster, and carried through thousands of people to a small room. The air was sticky and hard to breathe. I don't know how long I waited in that box, but the hours passed, and I was fed by a scared looking man. I felt weak and empty inside.

One day, as I woke up to my usual, cramped living quarters, the door opened and there, before me, stood my human mother. The door of my prison was wide open and I ran around excitedly, only pausing for my legs to collapse beneath me as I had not streched for so long. I was then parted from her and spent the next sixteen days in a strange-boarding house. Then she returned, and I was driven through mounds of traffic to what was obviously to be my new home. The rest of my family was there, and I was given as much attention as I could possibly absorb. I was back with the people I loved.

I never understood where I was or why I had come here, and I would often dream of the lovely garden I used to play in, and the tree I lay under in my home place. I could not decide if it would be better to be in the country I adored, or with the people I loved, but then, being a dog, I could not work out or understand such things.

The Foreign Service is at times a restless wandering, a dog's itinerant life, but we are always loyal like Argos although that is not always rewarded or appreciated.

A diplomat must always order new travelling boots. We venture through and across time zones. *To see things plainly you have to cross a frontier.*[1] Our ancestors could view seven parishes from their favourite mountain; our children must attend seven schools in seven different countries. You and the children are the forgotten envoys.

On the wall in front of me is a lithograph made at school by Lisa. It shows the root of a tree. Our children are part of two cultures, Norwegian and British. I grew up and got my education in Norway, you in England. The Foreign Service implied a transfer of their two cultures into a multicultural world. Inter cultural marriages and transcultural children have a particular bearing on national identity:

> They are perpetual outsiders ... flung into global jet streams by their parents' career choices and consequent mobility ... The children shuttle back and forth between nations, languages, cultures, and loyalties ... Growing up global, nomadic children often enjoy an extended worldview but may lack a particular national identity ... these children often feel as though they are citizens of the world and must grow to define home for themselves. They belong everywhere and nowhere ... and in their search for common ground, they often gravitate towards those whose childhoods have been similarly unrooted, often finding affinity in blended cultural groups. Even into adulthood, they are bound by perennial outsider status, by memories of frequent moves, and by the benefits and challenges a mobile childhood has granted them.[2]

You, from another country than mine, and our daughters Lisa and Nina, were the real pilgrims. You were travelling towards a future life *(peregrinus)* and you were always abroad *(perager)*. You transferred to new pastures, to new harbours and became part of all but unable to stay in one. You were international ships with ballast from former ports, tightrope dancers in the foreign service of Lilliput, vagabonds, voluntarily banished world citizens without a native land, *kikokushhijo mondai*[3] and *konketsuji*,[4] not permanently resident in one village or town, not in one country or even one continent, but always in a new school in a new country and a new continent, frequently at the airport waiting for the next aircraft, exodus from temporary homes where roots had wanted to grow further. The peripatetic life. Lisa illustrated this in a short story written in Tokyo after leaving Harare:

'What?' Nina and I screamed simultaneously. 'Japan?' I could not believe what I was hearing after three and a half wonderful years in Zimbabwe. The time had come once again for us to move to another corner of the world, but I just had not expected a place like Japan. It took me a long time to get used to that thought.

'Magic,' I said gently, 'I'll soon be leaving ... but this time it is going to be for good.' He pricked up his ears and looked at me searchingly. The thought of having to leave this wonderful pony I owned just pulled me to pieces. A dream I had as a child of having a pony had come to an end.

I saddled him up quickly and jumped on; his eyes shone, not with happiness, but with confusion – it is not easy to explain to an animal. I squeezed him softly and he moved off into a walk. Everything was so beautiful, so perfect where we lived. I wanted to live like this forever. The fun and competition of jumping, the show atmosphere that I so loved. It would be very difficult to live without it. The wonderful dreams I had of one day talking part in international show-jumping competitions seemed like shattered glass before me, not able to be picked up.

Only a few weeks earlier Magic and I, at long last, had our dream fulfilled by winning the C.D Championship and having received the champion rosette and trophy, we were now even more eager to improve – then, this news ...

We walked slowly out of the quiet, familiar yard and into a field which seemed to stretch for miles. The grass stood at six feet, coloured yellow from the scorching sun. It was so quiet and so perfect. I urged Magic into a canter; I could not imagine how I was going to live for years in a place I knew nothing about without the familiar Magic beneath me. How did it all start?

Magic was a rather special pony, he was a mystery. He had been found wild in the Inyanga Mountains. After several homes, I found him. He was a very healthy, handsome, bright golden chestnut gelding with a lot of scope.

The month we had to get ready to leave Zimbabwe went all too fast. The time came to find homes to look after both Magic and also Stormy, my sister's pony, while we were in Japan. Thankfully, we were able to leave our horses with people we already knew, but no reassuring could take away the pain of leaving him. I'll never forget that last gallop I had across the magnificient savanna. Later, as Magic walked up that ramp of the horsebox, I ran around and got in to say good-bye; the last good-bye, and as I did so, a tear fell from his eye. I slowly climbed from the box, and as the door was about to be closed, a soft grey nose pushed the door and rubbed itself on my hand as if to say 'Good-bye, don't stay away too long.' He looked so confused and worried. All my feelings exploded; I ran to the car and burst into tears.

As I watched from the car, I saw Magic turn his head and I heard a faint nicker. I would never forget the times we had shared together. Some day we might share them again ....
Then I saw the trailer disappear into the distance reflecting the African sun.

My face felt strained and my eyes were red as we drove along the main road to the airport. Everyone was silent, and memories flooded my brain. I turned around and looked out of the dusty window: I would miss my pleasant friends, the dust and all the wonderful places. I was going to miss Zimbabwe for a long, long time.

As the aircraft slowly lifted off from the ground, I waved good-bye to the place which had been my true home and to a pony which meant more to me than anything else in the world: Magic Streak.

We had stayed together as a family as Lisa and Nina attended the local schools in Harare and in Tokyo but the time came when they had to go to boarding school while we were still in Tokyo to preserve the continuity in education which the impending move from Tokyo would interrupt. Children and parents alike hate boarding schools, not always because of the schools, but because of the separation and distance.

On our last day in our last post in the diplomatic service Lisa sent us these words:

> You have instilled in us a sense of freedom. You have encouraged us to abandon the constraints put in place by society to restrict and tamper with one's very being. Flame trees, falling walls, chameleon wanderings, Eastern wisdom ... vivid dreams have found it hard to compete with reality. We have grown up to fit everywhere, but, essentially nowhere, which will always make us strange. Journeys can be solitary, but the unknown is embraced – perhaps there will be a place that brings everything together?

Perhaps never?

I did not tell you that I wrote a letter to the Foreign Ministry in 1999 about the unrewarded, dedicated role of the spouse. I referred to the attention given to family policy by the Ministry which had resulted in a special pension for the wives who accompanied their husbands at foreign postings and a family adviser in the Ministry. The pension was a recognition of the continuous, long and dedicated contribution in the service. In view of this I suggested that wives who had regularly played this part, including a period as an ambassdor's wife, be considered for a medal or even an order. I pointed out that the definition of Norwegian orders and medals are 'deserving calling for Norwegian interests' and 'contribution to the benefit of society'.

My suggestion, which went to the Permanent Secretary, was received with sympathetic understanding but with reservations. In other words: We do not wish to do this.

☐

In a double sense you dedicated your life to a foreign service. In no other profession is the wife so intimately involved with her husband's work and so visible. Marriage to a diplomat is a commitment not only to an individual but also to an entire way of life, to the vagaries of diplomatic life, its insecurities and discomforts and its privileges. Diplomatic wives lead a far more active role than that of a mere 'camp-follower' and it is the partnership angle which is the biggest blessing. Social life is part of the wider mandate of representing the country.[5] The diplomat's wife has traditionally been taken for granted but many continue to support the representative role of the ambassador. Gradually it is understood that wives may not be content to continue this role. An increasing number of joint (husband and wife) postings, the wife pursuing her own career and the wife being the diplomat, further changes the traditional system.

All foreign ministry officers regardless of rank get both retirement and death mentioned in the Ministry Bulletin. The death of the spouse is not mentioned. The forgotten, invisible, envoy.

TWENTY-FOUR

✦

You once said after retirement that you would like to go back one last time to all the places we had been together. We left it too long.

After you died I went back to Japan on a pilgrimage. Nina and I visited again the Embassy in 12-2, 5-chome, Minami Azabu, in Minato-ku where we had lived, the Sacred Heart School and the familiar streets.

Ise Jingu, Meteo-iwa and Byodoin Temple embody the essential spirit of rebirth found in Japanese mythology, culture and civilization – the rebuilding of the most sacred shrine and the rise of the phoenix, and the link between Shintoism and Buddism: 'In my own hands I hold a bowl of tea; I see all of nature represented in its green colour. Closing my eyes I find green mountains and pure water within my own heart. Silently, sitting alone, drinking tea I feel these become part of me.'[1]

We crossed the cypress Uji bridge over the sacred Isuzu river and visited Ise-Jingū (*Naigū* – the inner shrine – and *Gekū* – the outer shrine), the spiritual home of the Japanese people, the primate among the one hundred thousand Shinto sanctuaries. I tossed in a coin, took two deep bows, clapped my hands twice and bowed deeply again before the gate of the second outer fence of the main sanctuary of *Naigū* where the Sun Goddess is enshrined. The hills around, an area of more than five thousand hectares, are part of the sacred grounds. *Gekū* some distance away, enshrines Toyouke-no-Okami, the god of food, clothing and housing. The sacred buildings, in Shinto architecture built in the form of the traditional rice storehouse, may not be seen by the pilgrims but the metal-tipped poles protruding from the upper part of the gable at either end were visible against the blue sky.

Ise Jingu has been rebuilt sixty-one times since 690 A.D. in a construction ceremony called *shinigen* (a number of years) *sengu* (transferring the shrine). The shrine rotates between two identical sites, placed east west, every twenty years, most recently in 1993. The inspiration for the restoration comes from the worship of nature in Shinto, in particular the symbol of the rice crop which retains its form by renewal year after year.

The shrine is thus rebuilt and reborn to maintain the original purity and freshness of the design and to strengthen the harmony and blessing from the *kami* to the people of Japan and their reverence and respect for the imperial tradition. Even the Uji bridge is rebuilt. The wood from the old structures is used both to restore the *torii* at the entrance of the shrine and to distribute to other Shinto shrines in the country. In every sense the process is a symbol of renewal and of continuation. One hundred Shinto priests officiate in Ise and perform the various ceremonies and rituals, notably the transfer of treasures (first and foremost of the octagonal sacred mirror, *yata-no-kagami,* representing honesty) to the new site of *Naigū*. Most Japanese wish to visit Ise Jingū at least once in their lifetime.

We continued further to view Meoto-iwa, the twinned rocks in the sea half a mile off Futamigaura, south of Ise, the *kami* Izanagi and Izanami, the mythological creators of Japan. They are joined by a sacred straw rope (*shimenawa*) which is renewed every year in a special ceremony. We passed through the *torii* of the Okitama Shrine on the shore to see the *torii* on top of the largest rock silhouetted against the sky. A cave in this rock symbolizes the rock cave of heaven, the mythological essence associated with the Sun

Goddess and the bronze mirror. The sun can be seen rising between the rocks and in the distance Mount Fuji appears.

The journey took us to Uji between Nara and Kyoto, to the stone bridge over Uji river, a bridge mentioned in *The Tale of Genji* and one of the oldest bridges in Japan. I proceeded to the central remaining original building, the Amitabha Hall, renamed the Phoenix Hall in the Edo period, of the Byodo-in Temple. The whole building forms the image of a bird spreading its wings and a pair of phoenixes adorn the ridge of the central and main hall where the seated statue of Amida Tathagata and fifty-two Bodhisattvas are placed. The surrounding Pure Land Garden, a design which originated in the Heian period, adorns the buildings and the Phoenix Hall is reflected in the waters of the garden.

My publisher had a stand at the 13. Deutschsprachiger Japanologentag in Bonn in 2006 and my book on Germany and Japan was given a prominent position. I attended this conference that aimed to present the magnitude of German scholarship on Japan.

I found the way back to the village of Ippendorf and Neissestrasse where we had lived during our time in Germany.

It was a homecoming to a time past in Japan and Germany.

TWENTY-FIVE

✦

You did not get the chance to see your grandson. In a speech at his Christening in 2006, I said it did not make any sense at all that I was standing there and you had gone to the lands beyond the sea. I added that if your grandson were to possess your qualities if only by a thousandth part he would be one lucky boy when he grew up. 'Believe me, I know.' How you had wished to hold him in your arms.

Then I danced with you. 'I go back beyond the old man, mind and body broken, to find the unbroken man. It is the moment before the dance begins.'[1] We danced together in our grandson's honour. I played the song 'Love and happiness', appropriately from the record called *All the Roadrunning*,[2] and holding your young picture, the way you were when we danced together at the summer balls at Exeter and at Oxford, I danced with your spirit in an embrace to the grandson you could not embrace. It was a prayer. Your soul seemed to float free, a light aligned with my soul. I felt the pain of knowing what you were missing. *La dance des ombres,* the dance of the shades.[3]

'This existence of ours is as transient as autumn clouds. To watch the birth and death of beings is like looking at the movements of a dance. A lifetime is like a flash of lightning in the sky rushing by, like a torrent down a steep mountain.'[4]

The motion of the elements was seen as a great dance in the Renaissance and dancing was 'Love's proper exercise'.[5] This harmony between the universe and the soul, between love, music and dancing, has found the finest expression in Shakespeare's *The Merchant of Venice*:

> How sweet the moonlight sleeps upon this bank,
> Here will we sit, and let the sounds of music
> Creep in our ears; soft stillness, and the night
> Become the touches of sweet harmony:
> ...
> There's not the smallest orb which thou behold'st
> But in his motion like an angel sings,
> Still quiring to the young-eyed cherubins;
> Such harmony is in immortal souls.[6]

The dance of the elements, the music of the spheres when we met.

Lily, our first grandchild, does ballet now, like you did.

TWENTY-SIX

✦

I still haunt places you once stood.[1]

On our wedding anniversary, a sunny autumn day, I drove to Hythe and Lydd where we had spent the summers together in 1963 and 1964. I walked up Hillside Street to the Old Vicarage in Hythe where you had lived:

> And people who see me on my own
> As they pass me on the track
> Might wonder why, if I'm really alone,
> I pause sometimes and look back.[2]

I continued on the familiar road to the airport. The Bristols and Carvairs had long gone but a new Lydd Air with scheduled flights to Le Touquet and Lydd Aero Club training facility were in operation. The place looked much the same as I remembered it from those days in the sun.

To get closer to a world we used to know I took flying lessons from Manston Airport.

A year later I walked down Magpie Lane in Oxford towards the light of High Street and the eternal spires, to a memory of a time that we had shared.

Some things never change. I found you. I still search for you.

TWENTY-SEVEN

✦

I have come to the end of my letter to you. It has divided into twenty-seven fragments seen through a lens, darkly, black and white stills, seeking the movement and colour of your life.

I paused in the hall and glanced at the barometer. It read change. I gave the glass a light tap and the hand turned further down towards storm. This is how it had been since the day in January that changed everything. It was like tapping my own head and my mind read only change, a change that seemed to bend towards storm, a low pressure. Keeping the light, sunshine and fair winds forever away?

I opened my letter to literature (*litera* means letter) to reach for the soul of sorrow: 'To quote is to reflect on what has been said before, and unless we do that, we speak in a vacuum where no human voice can make a sound.'[1] I find myself trapped in a wilderness, in ten thousand leaves, to explain the inexplicable.

In the end there can only be a search for the essence of our life together. 'What time can never take from us is who we were in our best moments.'[2] The sense of loss does not go away, it is not diminished by time, it remains a constant flame and your absence reads like a letter without end, telling and retelling the story of our life.

'About suffering they were never wrong, the Old Masters.'[3] Such depth of feeling has been expressed again and again throughout human history and is mostly lost in silence; only a fraction is recorded and survives in poetry and prose. Each story of love and loss is unique, unmatched; it cannot be shared, we can only recognize that suffering is universal:

> We men are wretched things, and the gods, who have no cares themselves, have woven sorrow into the very pattern of our lives. You know that Zeus the Thunderer has two jars standing on the floor of his Palace, in which he keeps his gifts, the evils in one and the blessings in the other. People who receive from him a mixture of the two have varying fortunes, sometimes good and sometimes bad, though when Zeus serves a man from the jar of of evil only, he makes him an outcast ...[4]

The psychologists and psychiatrists would like us to believe that there are four stages of grief – shock, anger, depression and acceptance – as if we were talking about the four elements, the four seasons or the four ages of man. The soul has its own seasonal change. 'My grief lies onward, and my joy behind.'[5]

Ki No Tsurayuki, one of the collectors of poetry in *Kokinshū (Kokinwakashū)*, A Collection of Ancient and Modern Poems (about 905), wrote in a Preface:

> The Seeds of Japanese poetry lie in the human heart and grow into leaves of ten thousand words ... It is poetry which, without effort, moves heaven and earth, stirs the feelings of the invisible gods and spirits, smooths the relations of men and women, and calms the hearts of fierce warriors.[6]

The enduring power of poetry has been expressed most reverently in the *No* play *Sekidera Komachi*:

> The words of poetry will never fail.
> They are enduring as evergreen boughs of pine,
> Continuous as trailing branches of willow;
> For poetry, whose source and seed is found

In the human heart, is everlasting.
Though ages pass and all things vanish,
Poems will leave their marks behind,
And the traces of poetry will never disappear.[7]

Josephine Hart has expressed the same existential regard for poets, the gods of language:

Poetry, this trinity of sound, sense and sensibility, gave voice to experience in a way no other literary art form could ... it has provided me with a key to understanding; it has expressed what I believed inexpressible, whether of joy or despair ... It threw sudden shafts of light on my own soul and drew at least the shadow outline of the souls of others. It is the most ... that we are ever permitted to glimpse.[8]

Novalis perceived that *'die Liebe ist stumm, nur die Poesie kann für sie sprechen'* (Love is silent, only poetry can speak for love). The language of silence can only be bridged by poetry.

Goethe has reminded us that the function of poetry is to give us a second life in life.

The line 'A pity beyond all telling is hid in the heart of love'[9] is valued as one of the most beautiful in European love poetry. Is the heart of the matter of love only deep pity, tenderness in distress and suffering? In the heart of love there is a search for a word beyond telling even by the saints of language?

I add ten more leaves, reflections, in the search for the power of loss. At the end I am holding a cup of gold.

Twin compasses
Schiller's compelling early poem *Resignation* (1794) maintained in uncomplaining melancholy that *die Weltgeschichte ist das Weltgericht* (the world history is the world judgment). The reward of faith, belief, is just that:

Du hast gehofft, dein Lohn ist abgetragen,
Dein Glaube war dein zugewognes Glück,

111

Du konntest deine Weisen fragen:
Was man von der Minute ausgeschlagen,
Gibt keine Ewigkeit zurück.
(You have hoped, your reward is paid off,
Your faith was your allotted happiness,
You may ask your wise men:
What one has turned down from the moment
No eternity gives back.)[10]

The sudden and fatal attack that took your brain away made me wonder what consciousness is.

The festival of the British Association for the Advancement of Science on 5 September 2006 included studies and presentations on the paranormal including telepathy, consciousness and afterlife, phenomena that are considered impossible under the laws of physics.

The biologist, Rupert Sheldrake, has suggested that 'our minds may extend far beyond our brains, stretching out through fields that link us to our environment and to each other ... mental fields are rooted in brains but extend beyond them'.[11]

In the song, 'Sailing Round the Room', written by Emmylou Harris, the departed drifts out of her body and goes sailing round the room, out of the window to be 'a drop of summer rain' and 'birdsong when day is breaking.'

The out-of body-observation of (near) death experiences are being scientifically investigated in a rethinking of ideas about the brain and the mind. Is the mind separable from and not dependent on the brain? Is consciousness, the soul, independent of brain processes? How does matter become mind? We cannot see a thought.[12]

Neurologists at Stony Brook University in New York have proved with the help of MRI-scans that some couples exhibit a pleasure producing dopamine and display elements of limerence (the behaviour of new lovers) even after a long relationship.[13]

The cognitive scientist Douglas Hofstadter makes the point that the special bond created between two people in a long relationship is often so intense that when one dies the other soon follows. 'And if the other survives, it is often with the horrible feeling that half of their soul has been ripped out.' The sharing of so much between two people has aligned and fused their souls and in some dimensions of life turn them into a single unit that acts as a whole. The essence of a person, the soul or consciousness, the deeper aspects that give rise to a self, to an 'I', can be absorbed by another person's brain because the brain cells are not the bearers of consciousness. The brain, which at one level operates according to the laws of physics, gradually develops strange loops, curves, that float free and there are many loops of different sizes and degrees of complexity. The transmitters of consciousness are seen as *patterns* and these abstract patterns are the true seat of human consciousness, the 'I', the identity, the soul. One brain is inhabited to varying extents by other souls, and the personal identity is thus made up of fragments of identity of other individuals:

> But the key question is, no matter how much you absorb of another person, can you ever have absorbed *so much of them* that when that primary brain perishes, you can feel that that *person* did not totally perish from the earth, because they (or at least a significant fraction of them) are still instantiated in your brain, because they still live on in a 'second neural home'?[14]

Two people, who are very close, with the same pattern of hopes and dreams, create closely aligned souls, each of them lives partially in the other, and when one of them dies, the soul or consciousness lives on in the other person. Hofstadter realized after his wife's death that a 'core piece of her had not died at all, but that it lived on very determinedly in my brain', the manifestation of the interpenetration of souls.[15] The self or consciousness of the dead person may literally live on in the consciousness of the other. It was a fusion of two souls but how different was the preserved soul from the 'I' that had once flourished inside the brain of the deceased? The copy is inevitably incomplete but still present:

In the wake of a human being's death, what survives is a set of afterglows, some brighter and some dimmer, in the collective brains of all those who were dearest to them. And when those people in turn pass on, the afterglow becomes extremely faint ...

It takes a couple of generations for a soul to subside, for the flickering to cease, for all the embers to burn out ...

Though the primary brain has been eclipsed, there is, in those who remain and who are gathered to remember and reactivate the spirit of the departed, a collective corona that still glows. This is what human love means. The word 'love' cannot, thus, be separated from the word 'I'; the more deeply rooted the symbol for someone inside you, the greater the love, the brighter the light that remains behind.[16]

It occurred to me that Hofstadter had put forward a scientific idea of the labyrinth of consciousness that poets and writers have struggled with, felt and expressed from the earliest records of civilizations. It is a search that continues:

Whose soul was bent to mine like bending seaweed.[17]

On her leaned my soul.[18]

Our two soules therefore, which are one ... If they be two, they are two so as stiffe twin compasses are two ...[19]

Perhaps, when there is love, the widowed must stay for the resurrection of the beloved – so that the one who has gone is not really dead, but grows and is created for a second time in the soul of the living?[20]

When loved ones die, you have to live on their behalf. See things as though with their eyes.[21]

A shroud of memory grows
Between the two of them,
A tapestry of tides and tales.

One is the wave,
The other is the shore: An endless sea – a story of return.[22]

The long, passionate union ... a fantastic kingdom with its
own geography and language ...[23]

Uendelig nær er ditt smil, dine henders
Gave av jordisk ømhet
Uendelig nær er du alltid her
er de døde bestandig her og nu
i evig lys over hverdagens skritt
på jorden. (Endlessly close is your smile, your hands' gift of
earthly tenderness, endlessly close you are always here, are the
dead always here and now in eternal light over each day's
steps on earth.)[24]

Døden er forunderlig. Menneskene du elsket forlater deg
aldri. (Death is mystifyimg. The human beings you loved
never leave you.)[25]

Where do people go when they die?... it seems they simply
set up home inside our dreams.[26]

What will survive of us is love.[27]

I can feel Hailey so strongly that it momentarily stops the
breath in my smoke-filled throat and makes the hairs stand up
on the back of my neck ...[28]

I drive imagining you still at my side.[29]

I know why we try to keep the dead alive: we try to keep them
alive in order to keep them with us.[30]

There exists in the mind a tablet of wax, a gift given by
Mnemosyne, the goddess of memory, the mother of the muses.[31]
Mark Rowlands defines the special kind of memory of a past that
has written itself on you. It is in our lives and not in our conscious
experiences that we find the memories of those who are gone. The
most important way of remembering someone is by being the
person they made us. That is how we honour them.[32]

Consciousness, memory, imagination, reminiscence, metaphor: 'It is the two gifts combined, consciousness and memory, along with their abundance, that result in the human drama and confer upon that drama a tragic status ...'[33]

I have enscribed this letter to Lily, the granddaughter you held in your arms. The day will come when no one remembers the people who remembered you and I. But Lily will read the story and one day tell it to her grandchildren and they in turn may tell it to their grandchildren. Thus the mist of Angolême may still linger and flicker into time future?

The Blue Flower

To romanticize is to intensify the quality of feelings in such a way as to give the ordinary events a higher meaning, the everyday happenings a mysterious standing, the familiar the dignity of the unknown and the finite a sense of the infinite.[34]

Novalis's unfinished novel, the mythical romance, *Heinrich von Ofterdingen*,[35] the central work of German romaticism, explores the symbol and dream of *Die blaue Blume* (the light-blue flower), the colour of infinite distance 'das, was jeder sucht, ohne es selbst zu wissen, nenne man es nun Gott, Liebe, Ich oder Du' (that, which everybody searches for even without knowing it, be it God, Love, I or You).[36] The light-blue flower is love, longing and metaphysics. The search for the blue flower is our search for anything we want to achieve or understand. It is the sign for our constant discovery of the world around us. Sometimes we don't know what we are seaching for. Often we don't even know when we have found it.

It was after his beloved Sophie suddenly died that Novalis turned to writing. 'Sophie ist ewig Priesterin des Herzen' (Sophie is the eternal priestess of my heart). *Heinrich von Ofterdingen* is dedicated to Sophie.

Kawabata Yasunari, the first Japanese author to receive the Nobel Prize for Literature (1968), referred in his Nobel lecture to a short story in *Ise Monogatari* about the poet Ariwara no Yukihira who had decorated his home with blue wisteria to honour his invited guests. Kawabata sees in this image of wisteria something essentially Japanese and a symbol of the Heian culture – both gentle and reticent – and 'the poignant beauty of things long characterized by the Japanese as *mono no aware*'.[37]

Mono no aware

Buddhism teaches us, more bluntly and directly than any other religion, as the first noble truth, that suffering in life is inevitable, that all pleasures and good times are only temporary, and that sickness, the loss of loved ones, sorrow, grief, despair and death are waiting in the wings. 'But once again your storm says, ever so intimately: to live is to hurt!'[38] Human beings are powerless against *duhkha* (suffering) and *anitya* (impermanence), but Buddhism through three other noble truths defines the causes of suffering and suggests the law of *karma* to overcome the reality of suffering, detachment and renunciation as the road towards liberation and spiritual enlightenment.

The ephemeral nature of life and pleasure underpin Japanese aesthetic, spiritual and moral principles. The simplicity, tranquillity and patina of age of *wabi-sabi* lie at the heart of the tea ritual, the tea of *wabi* (*wabicha*), in Zen Buddhism.

There is affinity between the spiritual longing of *wabi-sabi* and the search for the blue flower in German culture.

Related to these concepts is the darker melancholy of *mono no aware* (the suffering of being). The expression *aware* in classical Japanese, either as hidden grief or as relief – the mythological reappearance of the sun goddess – lives on in the concept *mono no aware*.[39]

> Every time the word
> Aware comes out,
> Like dew settling on a leaf,
> My tears remind me longingly
> Of times now past.[40]

The novel *Genji Monogatari* (The Tale of Genji)[41] by Murasaki Shikibu, inspired by the Chinese poem *Chang-hen-ko* (The Song of Unending Sorrow) by Po Chu-i, is underpinned by the compassion, patience and pity of *aware*: the fleeting nature of life, the evanescence of beauty, human pleasure and happiness. These sentiments are hauntingly present in the novel, the love of Prince Genji for Yūgao and his memory of her, the desolation and tragic perspective and outcome.

Never regret

The fundamental difference in the use of tense in Chinese (and Japanese) compared with English has consequences for the understanding of love:

> 'Love', this English word: like other English words it has tense. 'Loved' or 'will love' or 'have loved'. All these specific tenses mean Love is a time-limited thing. Not infinite. It only exist in a particular period of time. In Chinese, Love is (*ai*). It has no tense. No past and future. Love in Chinese means a being, a situation, a circumstance. Love is existence, holding past and future.[42]

The Japanese concept *amae* (need-love or the dependency on another's love) which also describes the relationship between two lovers, does not have an exact equivalent in the English language although *amae* and romantic love in our Western culture may connect in a subtle way. When Oliver, after a quarrel with Jenny (in *Love Story*) says 'Jenny, I'm sorry,' she immediately retorts.' Stop. Love means not ever having to say you're sorry.' Why does Jenny interrupt his apology so urgently? Jenny in fact instinctively comes close to a Japanese understanding of love in refuting the words 'I'm sorry' because to the Japanese such sentiments do not reassure but disturb. In the psychology of *amae* 'those who are close to each other ... do not need words to express feelings.'[43] It is significant that Jenny's retort 'Love means not ever having to say you're sorry' was translated into Japanese as 'Love means that you never regret.' *Amae* and romantic love unite in a final embrace as Jenny asks Oliver not to feel guilty and not to blame himself for anything, in fact never to regret.

It would be so like you.

118

Alone
The grief that does not speak. Tony (in the short story 'Tony Takitani', by Murakami Haruki, and the film version directed by Ichikawa Jun) gives sorrow words through silence – *chinmoku* – knowing that he is destined to solitude after the fleeting moments with Eiko that made him feel alive for the first and only time in his life. He sits in Eiko's empty dressing room and stares at the walls. Tony feels the cosmic indifference, the absence of God and the spiritual void, the desolation. Only Eiko, his eternal love and soul's companion, had been able to remove the fog of loneliness from his heart. 'The only thing that remained tangible to him was the sense of absence.'[44]

> A face, bleached
> in the numberless night skies of the years –
> my face. Blue tears gradually light up.
> On the sea of your memory
> the wind whirls, raising up answers.
> The snow and the plum blossoms
> have all gone back to winter.
> Beyond the thousand mountains
> A setting moon shines in solitude ...[45]

But we are asked to wait, not to lose interest in everything, to listen to the music of pain, to our whole existence rehearsed by our sorrows, and to learn through suffering (*pathei mathos*). 'Wer auf sein Elend tritt steht höher' (He who steps on his distress stands higher).[46]

The French philosopher André Gorz and his wife Dorine, who was suffering from a terminal illness, committed suicide together in 2007. I can so easily understand when he writes: 'Je ne veux pas assister à ta crémation; je ne veux pas recevoir un bocal avec tes cendres ... Nous aimerions chacun ne pas avoir à survivre à la mort de l'autre' (I do not want to be there for your cremation; I do not want to receive an urn with your ashes ... Each of us would like not to survive the other's death).[47]

I had to do just that, the cremation, the urn and the survival.

André decided to seek Lethe and oblivion but if he had continued to live he would have carried her memory and her soul a little longer.

The hours inevitably carry me forward to shorten the time I have left to remember you, to keep your soul alive.

Searching

In Samuel Beckett's monologue play *Krapp's Last Tape* an old man, named Krapp, sits at the table in his den one late evening in the future, gets up, searches among his collection of tapes and finds, with a happy smile, spool five in box three and reads on the ledger: 'Equinox,[48] memorable equinox ... Farewell to – love' and starts the recording machine. He begins to listen to a recording he made as a much younger man, winds back and repeats the same passages over and over again, 'that memorable night in March, at the end of the jetty, in the howling wind, never to be forgotten, when suddenly I saw the whole thing. The vision at last ... The eyes she had!'[49]

His bleak, meaningless life is only restored for a fleeting moment when he plays the tape, the reminder of a love that he lost and he is left only with silence: *Extraordinary silence this evening .... Past midnight. Never knew such silence. The earth might be uninhabited.*[50]

Like Toni Takitani, Krapp has lost hope and the chance of happiness has gone forever. The desperate reach for some meaning is beyond his grasp but he is searching against all odds. The meaning is in the search – however meaningless.

Equinox – your birthday. Day and night are equal. I search and find the collection of old films and photographs from our memorable journeys and roads. I continue the search in silence.

Dustin Hoffman refers to photographs taken in the past: 'There you are, but really, there you *were*. It is like memory ... because you want it back. Because you want to do it again. Because ... you could do it better.'[51]

Music

The seventh seal had been opened. We play chess with Death and when we are not looking, he tricks us and we lose the game.[52] The dance of death.

Monsieur de Sainte Colombe, the seventeenth-century composer suddenly lost his beautiful wife. He recreated his sorrow in music of love and death, 'Le Tombeau des Regrets'. 'La musique est simplement là pour parler de ce dont la parole ne peut parler' (Music exists simply in order to speak of what words cannot express).[53]

'Music alone cuts through the barbed wire of language.'[54] The film director Ingmar Bergman spent his last years at Farø, grieving over the loss of his beloved wife and listening to music which had become 'a sort of gateway to other realities, different from those we can immediately perceive with our senses'. Bergman had no religious faith, but in music he heard the only possible evidence that there was something beyond this world.

The philosopher Ludwig Wittgenstein described Mozart and Beethoven as 'the true sons of God'.[55]

Hofstadter refers to Frederic Chopin's études for piano and how tiny fragments of the internal experiences of Chopin, his joys and sufferings, may be brought back to our brains through his music, how 'little fragments of his soul dance again'.[56]

Uncertainty

The Greek philosopher Heraclitus suggested that constant change, flow, flux, movement, is the very essence of nature. Nothing is permanent. We do not step twice into the same river because neither the river nor we are the same the second time. The river and we have inevitably changed.

A unique sense of beauty, implying a deeper understanding of change, perishability and the impermanence of all things, is fundamental to Japanese culture. The imagination expands beyond the cherry blossom at the very peak of its perfection to the early buds and the falling petals, from the promise of what is to come to the memory of what has been. The certainty of uncertainty does not close the spiritual search for beauty and perfection but enhances it into a seasonal change between past, present and future. Beauty is not separate from but modifies the frailty and the sorrow of existence:

> Are we to look at cherry blossom only in full bloom ... In all things, it is the beginnings and ends that are interesting. Does the love between men and women refer only to the moments when they are in each other's arms?[57]

The fragile condition of human life is seen as the very essence of beauty:

> If man were never to fade away like the dews of Adashino, never to vanish like the smoke over Toribeyama, but lingered on forever in this world, how things would lose their power to move us! The most precious thing in life is its uncertainty.[58]

A *tanka* (short poem) in *Kokinshu*, reminds us: *Yo no naka no uki tabi goto ni mi o nageba fukaki tani koso asaku nariname* (If in this sad world each time someone met with grief he cast himself from the highest cliff – even deep valleys would become shallow).

The Butterfly
In a Chinese legend the red azalea blossom is the symbol of the blood and the sorrow of love:

> There'll be a patch of azaleas
> blazing up from your eyes:
> the fiftieth time the perennial grasses
> make the change they can't help making:
> green to brown and back to green again.
> And I'll come looking for you
> – as a broken-winged and timid butterfly –
> and through a scent of tears, now red now white,
> with a touch so familiar
> I'll speak to you of a former incarnation ...[59]

122

A short time after you died, a wild butterfly, the *inachis io*, the most beautiful butterfly in the world, suddenly appeared in the sitting room seemingly out of nowhere as the doors and windows were shut.

I visited our daughter Nina in Phnom Penh in 2008 and we made a trip to Kep in the south-west of the country. One day a butterfly started to circle around me. It would not leave me and finally it sat down in the grass next to me. It then became very still and soon I saw that it had died. When I returned home I called my mother. Soon afterwards she died.

Had you come to warn me that my mother was about to die? Was the butterfly your loving soul, bearing a sign, sending a silent semaphore?

Are we not allowed to wonder at such things?

This old Japanese folk tale, a story of everlasting love, links the butterfly to the soul of the departed:

An old man named Takahama lived in a little house behind the cemetery of the temple of Sozanji. He was extremely amiable and generally liked by his neighbours, though most of them considered him to be a little mad. His madness, it would appear, entirely rested upon the fact that he had never married or evinced desire for intimate companionship with women.

One summer day he became very ill, so ill, in fact, that he sent for his sister-in-law and her son. They both came and did all they could to bring comfort during his last hours. While they watched, Takahama fell asleep; but he had no sooner done so than a large white butterfly flew into the room and rested on the old man's pillow. The young man tried to drive it away with a fan; but it came back three times, as if loth to leave the sufferer. At last Takahama's nephew chased it out into the garden, through the gate, and into the cemetery beyond, where it lingered over a woman's tomb, and then mysteriously disappeared. On examining the tomb the young man found the name 'Akiko' written upon it, together with a description narrating how Akiko died when she was eighteen. Though the tomb was covered with moss and must have been erected fifty years previously, the boy saw that it was surrounded with flowers, and that the little water tank had been recently filled.

When the young man returned to the house he found that Takahama had passed away, and he returned to his mother and told her what he had seen in the cemetery.

'Akiko?' murmured his mother. 'When your uncle was young he was betrothed to Akiko. She died of consumption shortly before their wedding day. When Akiko left this world your uncle resolved never to marry, and to live ever near her grave. For all these years he has remained faithful to his vow, and kept in his heart all the sweet memories of his one and only love.'

Every day Takahama went to the cemetery, whether the air was fragrant with summer breeze or thick with falling snow. Every day he went to her grave and prayed for her happiness, swept the tomb and set flowers there. When Takahama was dying, and he could no longer perform his loving task, Akiko came for him. That white butterfly was her sweet and loving soul.[60]

The sacred cup of gold
As I search among the myriads of poetic leaves I return to this poem. I wish to read it to you:

Es war ein König in Thule	There was a King in Thule
Gar treu bis an das Grab,	Faithful until his grave,
Dem sterbend seine Buhle	His sweetheart as she was dying
Einen goldnen Becher gab.	Gave him a cup of gold.
Es ging ihm nichts darüber,	There was nothing dearer to him,
Er leert' ihn jeden Schmaus;	He drained the cup at every feast;
Die Augen gingen ihm über,	His eyes filled with tears,
So oft er trank daraus.	Every time he drank from it.
Und als er kam zu sterben,	And as he was near the end,
Zähl' er seine Städt' im Reich,	He counted his towns in the land,

Gönnt' alles seinem Erben.	Gave everything to his heir,
Den Becher nicht zugleich.	Except the cup.
Er sass beim Königsmahle,	He sat at the Royal banquet,
Die Ritter um ihn her,	The knights around him,
Auf hohem Vätersaale	In the high ancestral hall
Dort auf dem Schloss am Meer.	There in the Palace by the sea.
Dort stand der alte Zecher,	There stood the old boozer,
Trank letzte Lebensglut,	Drank the last flame of life,
Und warf den heiligen Becher	And threw the sacred cup
Hinunter in die Flut.	Down in the incoming tide.
Er sah ihn stürtzen, trinken	He watched it falling, drinking
Und sinken tief ins Meer,	And sinking deep into the sea,
Die Augen täten ihm sinken,	His eyes began to close,
Trank nie einen Tropfen mehr.[61]	Never drank another drop.[62]

This is a poem about being faithful – not just faithful while both lovers are alive but remaining faithful after one lover has died, *gar treu bis an das Grab.* Love is understood in a religious context. The Cup is a sacramental symbol, *den heil'gen Becher*, and drinking from it is a sacred ritual, *so oft er trank daraus* (cf. *so oft ihr es trinket*).[63] The only life left is to use the cup in memory of the beloved.

The final throw of the cup from the palace high above into the deep water below is like a film in slow motion extending the perspective and creating distance and delay before the cup disappears in the waves. The sea is the symbol of eternity. The cup and the lover sink together in a final flight. The golden cup embracing the sea as he dies is an image of endless love.

You got up one morning and left.

Your name is Jill. You are my girl.

NOTES

✦

The *kanji* for four 囚 and death 死, although different, are both pronounced *shi*.

San in Japanese is a title of respect added to a name. (*Jillsan* developed as an affectionate nickname for Jill).

Chapter 1

1. Dante, *The Divine Comedy, Paradise,* Canto XXXI (l. 91–3), tr. by D. L. Sayers, Penguin, 1962, 329.
2. Dylan Thomas.
3. R.S. Thomas, 'A Marriage', *Do not go gentle*, Bloodaxe, 2003, 79.
4. Jacques Brel.
5. Shakespeare, *King Lear,* V, iii, l.273–4.
6. Kim Sowŏl (1902–34), 'The Old Stories', *Azaleas*, Columbia, 2007, 19.
7. Abu Al-Ala Al-Ma'Arri (973–1057), 'The Soul Driven from the Body', Bloodaxe, op. cit. 43.
8. *King Lear*, V,iii, l.310, 312.
9. Ibid. (l.309).
10. Cf. Dante, op. cit., 27.
11. The sacred shrine of Ise Jingū is rebuilt every twenty years.
12. Bjørnstjerne Bjørnson, 'Bergliot' ('Kjør langsomt, thi vi kommer tidsnok frem').
13. 'I woke to find myself in a dark wood, where the right road was wholly lost and gone.' Dante, *Hell,* Canto I.
14. Christina Rosetti, 'Remember', Bloodaxe, op. cit., 13.
15. Hinnøy, Nord-Norge, 68 degrees north.

16 Jeanne Willis, 'Inside Our Dreams', Bloodaxe, op. cit., 67.

17 Sigmund Freud, in a letter to Max Eitingen, 1929.

18 Edna St.Vincent Millay, 'Dirge Without Music', *In Loving Memory*, Little, Brown, 2004, 11.

19 John Barry, 'Out of Africa'.

20 E. Sartori, L.Quarantotto, in 'Romanza', Andrea Bocelli, 2001.

21 Margaret Cropper, 'I'll Hold Your Hand', *Something Understood*, BBC, 2001, 91.

22 Anon., 'Do not stand at my grave and weep', Souvenir Press.

23 Shakespeare, *The Tempest*, (IV, I, l. 156–7).

24 Ono no Komachi (ninth century), in *Kokinshū*.

25 Cf. Claudio Monteverdi's opera *Orfeo* (1607).

26 John Donne, 'The Sunne rising', op. cit., 59.

27 A Dialogue Poem in *1000 poems from the Manyoshū,* Dover, 2005, 285.

28 Nikos Kazantzakis, *Zorba the Greek*, Faber and Faber, 289.

29 Yehuda Amichai, 'The Place Where We Are Right'.

30 Dante, the last line in *Paradiso.*

Chapter 2

1 White nights, i.e. midnight sun in Japanese.

2 Elaine Feinstein, 'Another Anniversary', *Talking to the Dead*, Carcanet, 2007, 26.

3 Otomo Sukunamaro (eigth century) in *Manyōshū* translated by Harold Wright in *Ten Thousand Leaves*, Overlook Press, 1988, 78.

4 John Donne, 'A Nocturnall upon S. Lucies day, being the shortest day', *The Metaphysical Poets*, ed. Helen Gardner, Penguin, 1957, 69.

5 Last poem by Asano (Lord of the 47 *Rōnin*), 1701, in Emiko Ohnuki-Tierney, *Kamikaze, Cherry Blossoms, and Nationalisms,* Chicago, 2002, 148.

6 Norwegian language

7 Norwegian language

8 Cf. Ch. Twenty-one

9 George Eliot, *Middlemarch*, Ch. 20, Penguin Classics, 2003, 194.

10 In the Renaissance academic play *Pathomachia*.

11 Quoted in the film *Memoirs of a Geisha,* 2005 (based on the book by Arthur Golden).

12 A.E. Housman, XXX.

13 Pablo Neruda, Sonnet LXXXIX, *100 Love Sonnets*, tr. Stephen Tapscott, UTP, 1986.

14 Rupert Brooke, 'The Beginning', *Forgotten Treasures*, Daily Express, 2007, 6.

15 Ovid.

16 Shakespeare, *The Merchant of Venice,*V, i, l.242–3.

17 Umberto Eco, *The mysterious flame of Queen Loana,*Vintage, 2006, 448.

18 Pascal Quignard, *Tous les matins du monde*, Gallimard, 1991,60. Film by Alain Corneau, 2001.

[19] Anon. from *Manyōshū*, in *Ten Thousand Leaves*, op. cit. 81.
[20] Pamela Gillilan, from'When you died', *Do not go gentle*, Bloodaxe, op. cit., 51.
[21] Douglas Hofstadter, *I am a Strange Loop*, Basic Books, 2007, 227.
[22] Anon., in *Kokinshū*, Cheng & Tsui, 2004, 307.

Chapter 3

[1] Brigid Keennan, *Diplomatic Baggage*, John Murray, 2005, 10.
[2] Laws passed against Roman Catholics in Britain and Ireland after the Reformation.
[3] Ibid., 288.
[4] Vintage Classics, 2004, 108.
[5] 'An elegy on the death of his wife', in *Manyōshū*.
[6] Stephen King, *Lisey's Story*, Hodder and Stoughton, 2006, 15.

Chapter 4

[1] Jonathan Tropper, *How to talk to a widower*, Orion, 2007, 315.
[2] Dante, *La Vita Nuova XI*.
[3] I knew Novalis's unfinished novel *Heinrich von Ofterdingen* from my German studies; (see Ch. 27)
[4] Written about 910.
[5] Ernest Hemingway, *The Old Man and the Sea,* Arrow, 2004, 8.

Chapter 5

[1] C. P. Cavafy, 'Ithaka', 1894, (translated by Edmund Keeley and Philip Sherrard, *C. P. Cavafy. Collected Poems*, ed. George Savadis, Princeton University Press, 1992.

Chapter 8

[1] Cf. Ovid, *Metamorphoses.*

Chapter 12

[1] Kazantzakis, op. cit., 17.
[2] Gerard Manley Hopkins.

Chapter 15

[1] Japan's traditional puppet theatre.
[2] Novalis, *Heinrich von Ofterdingen*, 'Zueignung', Port Verlag, Stuttgart, 1949, 17.

Chapter 16

[1] Rupert Brooke, 1914.

Chapter 17

[1] Clint Eastwood in talks with Christopher Goodwin about *Flags of Our Fathers* and *Letters from Iwo Jima, The Sunday Times, Culture*, 10 December 2006.

Chapter 18

[1] *Kokinshū*, op. cit., 145.

[2] This is the first translation into English by Alexander Platt in *The Poems of Ludwig Uhland*, Leipzig, 1848.

[3] B. Gundersen, *Tysk for gymnasiet*, Brøggers forlag, Oslo, 1937, 62–3.

[4] Lucien Musset, *The Bayeux Tapestry*, The Boydell Press, 2002, 20–1.

[5] Andrew Bridgeford, *1066. The Hidden History of the Bayeux Tapestry*, Fourth Estate, 2004, 275–6. Carola Hicks, *The Bayeux Tapestry, The Life Story of a Masterpiece*, Vintage, 2007, 57.

[6] William Copeland Borlase, *The Descent, Name and Arms of Borlase of Borlase in the County of Cornwall,* George Bell & Sons, London, 1888.

[7] Samuel Murphy, *Grey Gold,* Moiety, 1996.

Chapter 20

[1] *Cadenus and Vanessa.*

[2] The Foreign Secretary, Maragaret Beckett, 'The modern FCO: the Myth, the Reality and the Future', speech at the FCO, 23.11.06.

Chapter 21

[1] Stephen Spender, 'To My Daughter', in Beverly Mcainsh (ed), *Something Understood*, Hodder & Stoughton, 2002, 84.

[2] Kris Kristoffersen, 'Loving Her Was Easier', 1970.

[3] Edward Fitzgerald.

Chapter 22

[1] By Alessandro Baricco, Canongate, 2006.

[2] Guy Lionnet, *The Romance of a Palm. Coco de mer*, L'ile aux images, 1986.

Chapter 23

[1] Salman Rushdie, *Imaginary Homelands*, Granta Books, 1991, 125.

[2] Faith Eidse and Nina Sichel (ed.), *Unrooted Childhoods*, nbi, 2004, 1–2.

[3] Returnee children after living abroad; *mondai,* problem.

[4] Mixed blood children.

[5] Katie Hickman, *Daughters of Britannia,* Harper Collins, 1999, 53, 54, 55, 67,103.

Chapter 24
[1] Soshitsu Sen (ed.), 'The Urasenke Tradition of Tea', The Urasenke Foundation.

Chapter 25
[1] Brendan Kennelly, 'I see You Dancing, Father'.
[2] By Mark Knopler and Emmylou Harris.
[3] Joan Didion, op. cit, 44–5.
[4] Buddha.
[5] Sir John Davies, *Orchestra*, 1596.
[6] Act V, scene i.

Chapter 26
[1] Emmylou Harris, *Not Enough.*
[2] Simon Bridges, 'Tomorrows', Julia Watson (ed.) *Poems and Readings for Funerals,* Penguin, 2004, 56.

Chapter 27
[1] Alberto Manguel, *The Library at Night,* Yale, 224.
[2] Mark Rowlands, *The Philosopher and the Wolf*, Granta, 2008, 237.
[3] W. H Auden, 'Musée des Beaux Arts'.
[4] Homer, *The Iliad,* XXIV Priam and Achilles, tr. By E.V. Rieu, Penguin, 1960, 451.
[5] Shakespeare, *Sonnet L*, 14.
[6] Laurel Rasplica Rodd and Mary Catherine Henkenius, *Kokinshū*, Cheng &Tsui Company, 2004, 35.
[7] Donald Keene (ed.), *Twenty Plays of the No Theatre*, (tr. by Karen Brazell), Columbia, 1970, 71.
[8] *Catching Life by the Throat*, Virago, 2006, 2–3.
[9] William Butler Yeats, 'The Pity of Love'; cf Graham Greene, *The Heart of the Matter.*
[10] My translation
[11] *The Times*, 6, 8 September 2006; cf. articles in *Science* and *Journal of Consciousness Studies.*
[12] Bryan Appleyard, 'The living dead,' *The Sunday Times Magazine*, 14.12.08
[13] *The Sunday Times*, 4 January 2009
[14] Douglas Hofstadter, op. cit., 236.
[15] Ibid., 270
[16] Ibid., 274.
[17] Kakimoto no Hitomaro, op. cit.
[18] Kakimoto, ibid., 43.
[19] John Donne, 'A Valediction: forbidding mourning', op. cit.
[20] Carson McCullers, *The Heart is a Lonely Hunter* (quoted in Hofstadter, op. cit., 258).

21 Louis de Bernieres, *Captain Corelli's Mandolin*.
22 Ioanna-Veronika Warwick, 'Penelope and Odysseus as One Person', *Something Understood*, BBC, 2001, 153.
23 Michel Chabon (writing about *Lisey's Story* by Stephen King).
24 Erling Christie, 'Døden er ingen avskjed', *Tverrsnitt*, Aschehoug og Gyldendal, 1958.
25 Siri Hustvedt, inteview in *Dagbladet (Magasinet)* 16 June 2007.
26 Jeanne Willis, 'Inside Our Dreams', *Poems and Readings for Funerals*, op. cit., 78.
27 Philip Larkin
28 Jonathan Tropper, *How to Talk to a Widower*, Orion, 2007, 34.
29 Elaine Feinstein, 'Winter', op. cit., 9.
30 Joan Didion, *The Year of Magical Thinking*, Fourth Estate, 2005, 225.
31 Plato, *Theaetetus*.
32 Mark Rowlqnds, op. cit., 46.
33 Antonio Damasio, *Looking for Spinoza,* quoted in Harriet Harvey Wood & A, S. Byatt, *Memory. An Anthology*, Chatto &Windus, 2008, 121.
34 Defined by Novalis.
35 Op. cit.
36 Ric. Huch, quoted in Dr. Leo Krell and Dr. Leonard Fiedler, *Deutsche Literaturgeschichte*, Buchners Verlag, 1960, 217.
37 J. Thomas Rimer and Van C. Gessel (ed.), *Modern Japanese Literature*, Vol. 2, Columbia, 523.
38 Zhou Mengdie, 'Scars', op. cit., 80.
39 Michael F. Marra, *The Poetics of Motoori Norinaga*, Hawai, 2007, 17–23; 172–200; Theodore de Bary (ed), *Sources of Japanese Tradition*, Vol. I, 172–4, Vol II, 4.
40 In *Kokinshu* (anon.)
41 About 1020.
42 Xiaolu Guo, *A Concise Chinese-English Dictionary for Lovers*, Vintage, 2008, 301.
43 Takeo Doi, *Understanding Amae*, Global Oriental, 2005, 67.
44 Published in Japan 1995, translated into English by Jay Rubin, *The New Yorker*, 2004, 14.
45 Zhou Mengdie, 'Prisoner', in Lloyd Haft, *Zhou Mengdie's Poetry of Consciousness*, Harrassowitz Verlag, 2006, 92.
46 Hölderlin *(Hyperion)*
47 *Lettre à D. Histoire d'un amour,* Galilée, 2006, 75.
48 Time when sun crosses equator and day and night are equal in spring, 20 March.
49 Samuel Beckett, *The Complete Dramatic Works*, Faber and Faber, 2006, 220, 222.
50 Ibid., 218, 223.

[51] *The Sunday Times, Culture*, op. cit.
[52] Cf. *Revelation* and Ingmar Bergman's masterpiece *Det sjunde inseglet* (The Seventh Seal), 1957.
[53] Ibid., 113.
[54] George Steiner, *My Unwritten Books*, Weidenfeld & Nicolson, 190.
[55] Bryan Appleyard, 'Why does music affect us like no other art?', *The Sunday Times, Culture*, 2 September 2007, 8–9.
[56] Op. cit., 10.
[57] Urabe no Kaneyoshi (Kenkō), *Tsurezuregusa*, 1330–33, in Donald Keene, *The Pleasures of Japanese Literature*, Columbia, 7.
[58] Ibid., 20.
[59] Zhou Mengdie, 'Prisoner', in ibid., 91.
[60] In F. Hadland Davis, *Myths and Legends of Japan*, London, 1913.
[61] Goethe's *Faust*, 2759–2782, Wegner Verlag, 1963, 89.
[62] My translation.
[63] I. Corinthians, 12 (this cup is the new testament in my blood ... as oft as ye drink it).

ACKNOWLEDGEMENTS

The author would like to thank the following for permission to quote:

University of Texas Press:
Pablo Neruda's 'Sonnet LXXXIX' in *100 Love Sonnets* by Pablo Neruda translated by Stephen Tapscott, 1986.

Dover Publications:
Extract from the poem 'After the Death of his wife' by Kakimoto no Hitomaro, in *1000 poems from the Manyōshū*, 2005 and extract from 'Dialogue Poem' 871–4, in ibid.

Harrassowitz Verlag:
The poem 'Prisoner', in Lloyd Haft's *Zhou Mengdie's Poetry of Consciousness*, 2006.

Columbia University Press:
Extract from the poem 'The Old Stories' in Kim Sowŏl, *Azaleas a book of poems*, 2007; and extract from the play *Sekidera Komachi* in Donald Keene, *The Pleasures of Japanese Literature*, 1988.

Lisa C. B. J. Cochrane for permission to quote her short story 'Magic Streek'.

Dr Nina H. B. Jørgensen for permission to quote her short story 'Toby's Travels' and the poem 'Shifting Sands'.